mandalas & meditations

for everyday living

52 pathways to personal power

Cassandra Lorius

CICO BOOKS

LONDON NEW YORK

This book is dedicated to Paul Standheven, energy healer, who supported me at a dark moment in my life. We initially worked on developing these meditations jointly, until the mandalas gave me a focus and frame for my life and held me in their magical circles.

This edition published in 2018 by CICO Books
an imprint of Ryland Peters & Small
20–21 Jockey's Fields, London WC1R 4BW
341 E 116th St, New York, NY 10029
www.rylandpeters.com

10 9 8 7 6 5 4 3 2 1

First published in 2008

Text © Cassandra Lorius 2008
Design and illustrations © CICO Books 2008

A CIP catalogue record for this book is available from the British Library

ISBN: 978 1 78249 575 8

Printed in China

Editor: Alison Wormleighton
Designer: David Fordham
Illustrator: Melissa Launay

mandalas &
meditations
for everyday living

Contents

INTRODUCTION: MANDALAS, CIRCLES OF WHOLENESS

A MANDALA IS A pattern of power that represents the whole circle of existence. Its circular shape encloses a depiction of a holistic cosmos. Mandala shapes naturally occur in the organic world; their perfect forms can be seen in atomic structures, crystals and flowers, as well as solar systems and wave forms. I like the description by the Mandala Project (an online gallery) of a mandala as a primal circular pattern that has existed in nature since the beginning of time.

SPIRITUAL JOURNEYS

Anthropologists have discovered that representations of mandalas have long been used in many cultures as vehicles for shamanic journeys. Navajo Indians, for example, created sand mandalas which described journeys into the spirit realm in a similar way to the Aboriginal bark or rock paintings of dreamtime. Among the Navajo, sand paintings were completed by the medicine man, who used them in healing rituals. I have seen fabulous photographs of a shamanic ritual conducted with a young boy sitting inside a section of the sand map, used for a therapeutic rite designed to banish disease.

LEFT: *"Dance" (page 67) depicts Lord Shiva, who dances the world into creation.*

Above & right: "Looking" (page 57) depicts the third eye. "Connecting with the Cosmos" (page 68) invites us to release stuck emotions.

Mandalas can be used as a path to power, describing an inner journey to the center. The center is both a point of focus and the source of creation—represented in Indian mandalas as a primal dot (bindi) in the center.

Many cultures have a tradition of using painted or made images in mandala designs during rituals to facilitate altered states of consciousness. These are used as circles of empowerment. Therefore, a wider definition of mandalas is that they are holistic diagrams encompassing a spiritual approach to self-development, healing and growth.

TANTRA AND TANTRIC BUDDHISM

Traditional mandalas are particularly associated with tantric Hinduism and Buddhism. For millennia, Hindu tantrics used geometric designs called yantras to symbolize a spiritual understanding of reality. The author Ajit Mookerjee describes them as "thought forms". They are not merely representations of the transcendent realm but depict potential energies that can be processed during meditation practice. Within tantra there are also invocation practices known as mantra, which involve repeating words or sounds.

ABOVE: *A mandala made from flower petals to celebrate the Onam festival, which takes place every autumn in Kerala, India.*

LEFT: *Detail from the Shri yantra ("Divine Love", page 30).*

In mystical traditions, sacred texts are read as metaphors, alluding to inner states of mind as opposed to the outer experience of reality. Now that we have digested some of this precious material in our own culture, we can spell out the psychological dimensions of spiritual texts and apply them in a variety of valuable ways.

WHAT IS TANTRA?

The Sanskrit word tantra has a multiplicity of meanings, referring to texts and practices that weave threads of connection between texts and lived experience. They also refer to rituals that enliven our energy body and incorporate it into meditation and other spiritual practices. Tantra utilizes our sensory experience of living in a body to facilitate transformation, rather than denying the body and its desires as so many other traditions do. In fact, a tantric perspective is that embodying change and living through emotional and psychic transformation provides a fast track to enlightenment.

Tantra comprizes a collection of pre-Hindu traditions that are now also woven into the Vajrayana school of Tibetan Buddhism. The very different attitude to the relationship between divine and human is most clearly seen in the practice of deity visualizations. In deity practices you focus on a god or goddess whose qualities you aspire to emulate, and imagine that their body merges with your own, so you can incorporate their divine qualities. This is a unique method to power your personal development, and so I have developed a deity meditation for you to explore in this mandala collection (see page 77).

MYSTICAL MANDALAS

All mandalas depict spiritual planes of reality. Tibetan Buddhists use them to map sacred abodes of the gods, Buddhas, bodhisattvas (aspiring Buddhas) and dakinis (sky-dancers), within which infinite wisdom and compassion are manifested. Some mandalas illustrate the obstacles that have to be overcome in order to cultivate compassion and wisdom; these are often depicted in the form of terrifying demons. I have developed a meditation to help you transform your own inner demons (see page 65) which come in the form of negative emotions. Meditating on your psychological journey gives you food for thought about your own personal limitations and resistance to change.

Another lovely ritual use of mandalas is the Tibetan practice of designing and creating elaborate sand mandalas, such as the Kalachakra. Part of the purpose of this esoteric ritual is to demonstrate the impermanence of our present lives and physical condition. When monks wash away the beautiful and highly intricate mandalas that have taken many days to create, they believe that this dissolves the energy created through spiritual practice and releases its merit. By mixing the sand into rivers and oceans, this merit spreads through them and benefits the world. In 1973 the spiritual head of Tibetan Buddhism, the Dalai Lama, first permitted monks to make the Kalachakra "Wheel of Time" sand mandala in public. This intricate mandala has long been used for tantric initiation.

LEFT: *Buddhist monks use sand to create a mandala. After completion, the sand will be placed in a stream to spread the mandala's spiritual blessing.*

ABOVE: *A sixteenth-century Tibetan mandala depicting Buddha Vairocana. The geometric devices of a cross, a square in a circle, the four corners and an inner ring of lotus petals show how existence can embrace polarities.*

OUTSIDE THE EASTERN TRADITION

Mandala patterns are also found in non-Eastern mystic traditions. They can be seen in the rose windows of cathedrals such as Chartres and Notre Dame, both dating from the thirteenth century, which inspire us with their beauty and transcendent power. A rose window was the inspiration for the Grace mandala on page 122.

Through the centuries, mandalas have informed the work of mystics, such as the twelfth-century nun Hildegard of Bingen. In her illustrated book *Scivias* she published

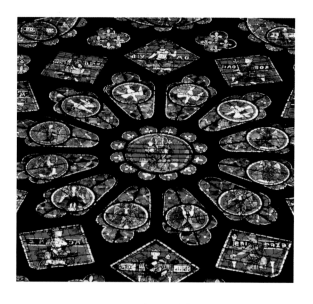

ABOVE: *The north rose window at Chartres cathedral, France, dating from 1223.*

LEFT: *An image taken from* Scivias, *by Hildegard of Bingen, illustrating her vision of a choir of angels.*

visionary mandalas depicting circles of angelic beings in celebration of God's creation.

Similar rituals are found in ancient traditions. For instance, the labyrinth, a maze-like pathway that could be literally walked to gain power and insight, is found in many cultures around the world. The classical labyrinth is thought to date back several thousand years, while a more complex version became popular during the Middle Ages, and labyrinths still exist in the floors of many European churches. The most famous, dating back to about 1200, is at Chartres, where the walking of the labyrinth won as much spiritual merit as going on the established, church-sanctioned pilgrimage to Jerusalem. Walking the labyrinth would appear to be an expression of a basic human need for wholeness.

The hajj, the Islamic pilgrimage to Mecca, involves seven circumambulations of a central building, the Ka'ba, the holiest place in Islam. This square in the middle of a circle can be seen in mystical terms as symbolically reconciling a man-made geometrical shape with the universal and holistic shape of the circle.

Among the Sufi orders, the Mevlevi dervishes, also known as whirling dervishes, use the ritual of a whirling dance as a means of prayer. Their spinning circles symbolize the elliptical orbits of planets around the sun.

ABOVE: *"Grace" mandala (page 123) is an example of sacred art based upon geometry. This mandala was inspired by the intricate stained-glass designs of cathedral rose windows.*

A HOLISTIC WORLD

Within traditional cultures, from Navajo to Tibetan, mandalas are used to help attune man's awareness to his place in a holistic world, and these indigenous traditions have been mined for decades by Western spiritual practitioners. The pioneer of this approach was the Swiss psychological explorer and psychotherapist Carl Jung (1875–1961), who encouraged his clients to regularly paint their own mandalas.

Jung noticed that his clients generated their mandalas from their own unconscious—even where they had had no previous contact with traditional mandalas. Because these forms have arisen in many disparate cultures over millennia, emerging spontaneously in dreams and drawings, Jung came to the conclusion that mandalas were universal archetypes. He considered each individual's artwork to be a personal manifestation of a collective unconscious common to all humanity.

THE SELF AND INDIVIDUATION

Jung saw mandalas as an archetypal expression of our own personal journey to self-development. According to psychoanalysts, personal growth is the most compelling goal in life, once basic survival needs have been satisfied. Jung found mandalas an extremely potent means of self-development, and he used this method effectively with his clients, demonstrating how each person's mandalas evolved and were transformed over years of work.

Jung saw the ideal world contained within a mandala as representing an integrated world and he claimed that a mandala functions as a guide to becoming integrated. He saw the mandala as symbolizing the perfect wholeness of the self. In *Man and his Symbols*, Jung described the practice of making a mandala as a way to integrate scattered parts of oneself, creating a center and coalescing into a unified whole around this center.

Each of us has a "story" that we tell about ourself—it makes up our identity. Jung believed that if our personal reality has been denied by our family and schooling or has been rejected by others

ABOVE & LEFT: The journey of the self. The human figure has a rainbow body, which projects into the environment. The Childhood mandala (page 103) is used for integrating aspects of the past.

(or ourself), we risk psychological disintegration. Although he believed that a human being is inwardly whole, he felt that most of us have lost touch with important parts of ourselves. Rediscovering our own story will facilitate healing and integration. Through exploring the symbolic messages of our dreams and active imagination, we can rediscover and reintegrate our different facets.

The goal of life, according to Jung, is a type of self-realization which he called individuation. Jung described it as the process of getting to know, expressing and making constructive relationships between the various components of the self. We all have a specific nature that is uniquely our own, and unless this is fulfilled through a union of our conscious and our unconscious, we may become unbalanced or ill. If we can recognize and accept our uniqueness, we can embark on a process of individuation and tap into our true self. We do not have to be content with our limited horizons but can reach a higher state of consciousness. Jung believed that this journey of transformation is at the mystical heart of all religions.

THE STARTING POINT

Jung's approach is the starting point for this book. The artwork and imagery that individuals generate from their unconscious are particularly valid for us, and the mandala forms that contemporary artists generate are also very relevant. Melissa Launay, the artist, and I have developed highly personal interpretations of the theme of mandalas, freely drawing on the iconography and associations of more traditional mandalas while finding our own expression. Many contemporary artists are likewise using mandala patterns and principles to create inspirational art, incorporating elements of balance and harmony to create an inspiring whole.

We offer these meditations and mandalas as the starting point to stimulate your own journey of integration, or to inspire you to create your own. We share the belief that creating or meditating on mandalas provides an opportunity to nurture these qualities in ourselves, and I trust that some of the themes I have chosen to develop are relevant to your needs right now.

MEDITATING WITH MANDALAS

LEFT: *A "Compassion' mandala (page 34) shows the goddess Tara holding a lotus flower, the symbol of transformation.*

LEFT: *Meditation can help to connect and balance the body's seven principal energy points, or chakras, shown in this "Chakra' mandala (page 83).*

IN THIS CHAPTER, I have suggested a few simple techniques to help you develop the ability to meditate. Most teachers say that it doesn't come easily straight away, and that it requires practice to create a habit. Making a regular time to meditate may help you to cultivate the right state of mind. Either work through all the meditations in this book, using one mandala to focus on each week throughout the year, or simply pick and choose those that appeal to you most. We have used a range of symbols and styles in case you find some more accessible than others. Many people respond well to affirmations, and so I have taken care to keep the meditations in this book positive and to use affirmation. After reading the meditation you may wish to spend between 10 and 30 minutes gazing at the mandala, letting the words work on your imagination, or allowing the images to lead you deeper into your own personal journey.

METHODS OF CONTEMPLATION

Lead us from untruth to truth
Lead us from darkness to light
Lead us from death to immortality
Aum, let there be peace!
—*Vedic chant*

ACCORDING TO THE singer Chloe Goodchild, meditation comes in different ways: it can come through the naked voice, the liberated body, the penetrating vision, the empty mind, the loving heart, or the ecstatic embrace—a particularly tantric means of transformation.

These mandalas present inspiration for meditation in a visual form. We all respond in different ways to visual stimuli and have our own styles of processing information, and these individual preferences can be incorporated into the mandala-making and meditations. For some of us the kinaesthetic sense—the awareness of our body's position and movement—is especially strong, so you may find that moving around frees your creative mind. For most people sensory experience is important, so if touch, sound, smell or taste is evocative for you, you may wish to incorporate it in your mandala-making and your meditation. That is why some people use humming, incense or essential oils to facilitate altered brain states.

ABOVE & LEFT: *"Deity Practice" (page 76), showing an angel and heart, provides a template for us to aspire to, while "Invocation" (page 120) is an interpretation of the sound of creation.*

ACCESSING A MEDITATIVE STATE

I have included different styles of accessing meditative states, so that you can choose the methods that suit you best, but you may find that one or more of the following approaches particularly suit you.

Ways to Access a Meditative State

● The traditional method used by Buddhists is visualization. Summon up a visual scenario in your mind's eye, and let the scene unfold. You may impose your own narrative, or the one suggested by the meditation. See where it takes you.

● Record the meditation so you can follow the sound of your own voice. It's important to speak slowly in order to allow yourself space to think during playback.

● Consider using these mandala meditations with a friend or partner, or even a small group. Some people focus better in a group setting, and the relationship with others serves to intensify or to reflect back changes within.

● Take a word or a theme, read the meditation, or perhaps a poem, and then reflect on it. Examine its personal relevance and meaning, and freely associate on the theme.

● Use a mantra—constantly repeat a phrase or a single word, such as "compassion". Repeating the mantra pulls your awareness back to the theme you are working on.

● Recall a situation that has evoked particular feelings. Once you have summoned up the emotions, they can be transformed into positive feelings and directed toward other beings. For instance, in the classic Buddhist meditation on loving kindness (see page 36), you project positive emotions to different groups of people. The feelings are projected out universally, to everyone, regardless of your relationship with them.

WHAT DOES MEDITATION INVOLVE?

Meditation refers to an altered state of consciousness. This can be described in a host of ways, but often either as a mental quality or an emotional experience. Words used to describe states of meditation include awareness, clarity, centeredness, stillness, equanimity, calmness, fullness, love, compassion, connectedness, bliss, sublime, light… the list is endless.

Practicing meditation often brings profound changes within weeks—you feel calmer, more centered, more patient, less anxious. Your sleep is easier and you awake refreshed. Your concentration improves and you feel happier and more confident. As you become calmer, you are less agitated and more focused. You are also more in touch with your intuition, because your controlling mind stops

ABOVE: *"Bliss" (page 50) refers to the dynamic energy felt when you let go.*

interfering so much. You instinctively know what is the most appropriate thing to say or do—and when it's better to leave things alone. As your energy increases, you access your spontaneity and liveliness. You are more psychologically buoyant in your response to challenges. All these changes are key to well-being, as they increase energy, lower blood pressure and banish depression, boredom and frustration.

You might also become more socially attractive, because other people enjoy being with a positive, happy person. In addition, when you feel more connected, you connect more easily. Increased self-knowledge and understanding of others lead to better connections. If you become more self-accepting, you develop tolerance and compassion for others. If you cultivate sympathy, you feel more empathy. In turn, those around you respond more favorably, reinforcing the changes you have made.

ABOVE, RIGHT & FAR RIGHT: *"Forgiveness" (page 38) for inner peace; "Laughter" (page 59) for simple enjoyment; "Pain" (page 110) explores ways of dealing with pain, using the healing symbol of the caduceus.*

MEDITATION AND EMOTIONS

The place to start working on integration and development is within yourself. You can use meditations to detox negative emotions, helping you to become more optimistic and attract more positive experiences into your life. You can also use meditation to reduce and clear your entanglements with the past and your worries about the future. You can choose to change negative habits by creating positive affirmations, training your mind into more healthy habits that foster well-being.

Emotions are just a particular form of energy, and you can choose what kind of energy you want in your life. Is righteous anger more appropriate than forgiveness? Do you want to reclaim your right to express your inner voice through mantra, or words of power? Do you want to reignite your passion for life? If so, try a fire meditation to increase your passion and energy. Or use a laughing meditation if you wish to encourage your whole body to "lighten up". Unhappiness is as subjective as happiness and is about how you see things. You can choose to redirect your energy by making choices. You can change the habit of unhappiness, which may have been inculcated very early in your life.

MEDITATION AND SPIRITUALITY

You can use mandala meditations as a journey of self-discovery, or self-transformation. In Eastern traditions, awakening is only the beginning of the spiritual process. Awakening has been known by many different names—nirvana, consciousness, the Kingdom of Heaven, Buddha nature or enlightenment. The first sign of awakening is "entering the stream"—becoming aware of the existence of a spiritual dimension to life. Many experienced meditators achieve a sense of freedom, moments of bliss or a feeling of letting go, on accessing this deeper awareness underlying everyday reality. Just empty your mind of thoughts and preoccupations in order to open yourself to this experience.

The spiritual path is best described as a spiral progression, rather than a linear one, and after periods of heightened experience it can be a struggle finding your way back to this satisfying awareness. Within Eastern traditions the four strong traditions of spiritual journey (or yoga) listed below seem relevant to us.

The Traditions of Spiritual Journey

- The path of oneness—a desire for unity with the beloved.

- The path of identification with emptiness—experiencing the spaciousness behind the distractions of daily life.

- The path of suffering—where after tremendous pain, grief, loss or illness we experience the possibility of redemption or transformation.

- The path of being in the continuous present, in which we inhabit our bodies, our lives, our senses and our relationships fully. This is part of the tantric way.

These above traditions relate to different meditation styles. I am mindful of the differences in developing these meditation practices for weekly exploration; some may appear to be more effective than others. Stay with what works for you and develop your own meditation style.

Meditation practices help us to go inward to uncover who we really are. Mandalas remind us that we already have the seeds of spiritual awakening inside—it is just a matter of moving attention away from the periphery to the center. They remind you of the power and beauty of your inner reality.

Focus your mind on the wholeness of life and the amazing web of interconnections that impact on so many areas of your life, which can be so helpful and timely in moving life along. In aligning yourself with an underlying spiritual dimension, welcome this energy into your own life, nourishing your thoughts and desires, so that spirituality manifests in a way that is personal to you. Let it shape your life. This reality is first expressed in your thoughts and desires, and then manifested in the world.

Meditation connects you with the source of unconditional love and enables you to open yourself to receive so much more love. Regular meditation shows you the true nature of existence, which mystics describe as divine love. Meditation is the door through which you enter these altered states of consciousness.

ABOVE & RIGHT:
"Connecting with the Cosmos" and "Karma" (pages 68 and 131) broaden our outlook.

PREPARING FOR MEDITATION

Prepare your body if necessary, as explained below. Settle yourself down in front of the mandala and gaze at it. You can either take in the whole mandala, or start with the center, seeing if the image in the center has relevance or meaning to you. Watch your thoughts, or pay attention to any changes or responses in your body, whether postural or a movement of energy. Let your eyes travel where they will, settling on any aspects of the mandala that are evocative for you: the colors, forms, patterns or symbols. You will not need to analyse the shapes—they should stimulate your own personal processing. Use the text in the same way, resting your awareness on any words, phrases or sentences that seem relevant to you.

RELAX

If you feel fatigued, tense or weak, the resulting aches and discomfort can affect your ability to focus attention on your internal state. Combat this by stretching and releasing muscle tension, as well as developing stamina and strength to support your body while sitting upright and still. This exercise may be a helpful preliminary to other meditations, because in order to build energy or process emotions your body should be relaxed and open. Lie on the floor to allow your body to let go of body armoring and physical tension as much as possible. It may take some time to work through layers of physical armoring.

Relaxation Exercise

1 Start in a standing position. Stretch slowly and gently, breathing deeply and steadily as you focus on letting go of physical armoring. Let your head gently drop forward to lengthen your neck. Roll your head from side to side to stretch out tight muscles, using your breath to help you release. Breathe out tension from the part of your body you are working on. Once your neck feels more comfortable, let go of tension in your face, relaxing the jaws in particular, then let go of remaining tension in your muscles.

2 With your head up, slowly stretch your arms upward and then sideways, lengthening the muscles along the side of your body. Focus on releasing tension and discomfort rather than trying to extend your movements.

3 Sitting on your haunches, stretch your legs out in front, keeping your back straight, then slowly bend slightly forward. Keep breathing and focus on lengthening your lower back, letting go of discomfort, rather than on getting your torso near the floor!

4 Lie down to work on releasing tension in your abdomen. With your hands on each side of your torso, stroke the area just under the rib cage, starting in the center and tracing the curves out to the side of the body. Use long, sweeping strokes with some pressure but without causing discomfort. You can use two fingers in a walking motion to lightly massage along the bottom edge of the ribcage, from the center outward. Then use similar long, sweeping strokes from the middle of the diaphragm (where the bottom of the ribcage starts), downwards toward the pubic bone.

5 Once your physical tension has eased, reposition yourself in a sitting position on the floor. Now slowly lie down, letting the small of your back go down first and unfurling your spine as you do so and allow it to lengthen and increase the space between the vertebrae. Let your ribcage expand and your pelvis widen. Bring your knees up, leaving your feet on the floor, so that your lower back can lengthen. Feel as though you are sinking into the floor as you settle into a feeling of spaciousness and ease in your body. Widen the space between your shoulders, and lengthen your neck, releasing the tension—breathe it away.

6 Allow your body to get more and more comfortable. Let it become heavy with relaxation on the floor. Enjoy letting go. Rest in this posture for 10–20 minutes. Your back is straight and you have let go of tension, which could have been blocking the flow of energy. You may now feel the energy moving more freely around your body.

ENERGIZE

The simplest way of energizing is lying on the floor from this position described below. Lie on a mat because you will be bouncing your body up and down. Alternatively, you can stand and shake your whole body (see step 3).

Energizing Exercise

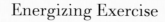

1 From lying with your knees up and your arms along the sides of your body, lift your pelvis, taking the weight on your lower legs and supporting your upper body with your arms, so that your shoulders don't crunch up with tension again.

2 While you breathe deeply into your abdomen, jiggle your pelvis up and down, and side to side. Feel the small movement energizing your pelvis, stomach, chest and legs. Let the dynamic movement become larger, energizing your whole body.

3 Alternatively, to energize from a standing position, stand with your knees slightly bent and shake your pelvis for a few minutes. Gradually let this movement climb and spread through your whole body, so that it awakes and stimulates you. Don't forget your arms, hands, legs and feet. After shaking for several minutes (perhaps to some rhythmic music), let your voice join in, humming or singing. Stand or lie for a while, feeling your body humming with energy.

ABOVE LEFT, ABOVE RIGHT: *In certain Buddhist traditions, wisdom (page 46) is depicted as masculine and compassion (page 34) as feminine. Both are necessary for spiritual growth.*

FAR RIGHT: *In the mandala for healing (page 71) the lotus in the pelvis is a symbol of transformation.*

BREATHE

After energizing your body you can turn your attention to the movement of the spirit in your body, through breath. Breath and spirit are closely linked—the Arabic *ruh*, the Hebrew *ruach* and the Latin *spiritus* all mean both breath and spirit.

Breathing Exercise

1 Once you have settled into a relaxed state, concentrate on how you breathe, without trying to alter it or control it. Notice the rhythm your breathing follows, and the inevitable variations in pace and length of breath. Observe how your body responds as you breathe in. As your breathing continues its cycles, does your attention stay on your breath or does it wander off? Maintain your concentration on your breath, and follow your inhalation into the lungs, like a wave that moves through your chest and diaphragm into your belly. Keep your shoulders and belly relaxed as you focus on the passage of your breath.

2 In following your breath, you can narrow the focus of your attention to the part of your body that it is passing through. Be your nose as the air enters, then be your windpipe as the air passes through. Be your lungs as they expand, and be your belly if you feel the wave extending that far.

3 Notice the point at which your intake feels complete and satisfying. Before your next breath, be aware of the gap between it and the last breath, before allowing your attention to flow upward with the breath. Focus on this flow inward with the breath, the gap, and the flow outward.

AWARENESS

The Zen Buddhist Thich Nhat Hanh describes emptiness as full of everything and empty of nothing. Mandala meditations are aimed at cultivating an awareness of this dual nature of reality, which consists of both form and emptiness.

FORM REFERS TO our everyday world of homes, family, work and money. Emptiness refers to the pure energy that fills each and every form, and that exists regardless of form. A good way of tapping the awareness of the pure energy of life is to engage totally with the present. This will encourage your identification with structure, familiar routines, or the details of the form your experience takes to drop away.

The detailed work on this mandala inspired by a Celtic shield draws your eye into its proliferating circles and flowing lines. Focusing on this detail will help you develop your ability to concentrate, thereby improving your awareness.

  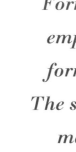 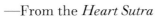   

Form is emptiness, emptiness is form;
emptiness does not differ from form,
form does not differ from emptiness.
The same is true of feelings, perceptions,
mental formations, consciousness.

—From the *Heart Sutra*

MEDITATION ON AWARENESS

1 Adopt a sitting pose. Sit comfortably with a straight back. If you are flexible you may be able to sit cross-legged. Use a wall to support your back if necessary.

2 Whether the sensations that arise in your body and psyche are pleasurable or painful, give them the attention they need. Go into the experience even more deeply, and once you have savored their quality, just let them go.

3 Practice being totally present, alert, aware of what is going on around you. If thoughts distract you, just notice whatever script is running through your head. Let it run without comment or judgment.

4 Tune into your emotions but be aware that they are not you. Separate your self from your emotional reactions. Notice your reactions, and then let them go.

5 Be open to growth. Allow change. Just as the pace and sound of your breath constantly varies, allow your internal processes to ebb and flow, without trying to control them.

ENGAGING WITH THE PRESENT

Meditation is a process of staying in the continuous present without being over-attached to what occurs. Another word for it is "mindfulness"—being fully conscious of whatever is going on around you. The more you practice awareness, the easier it will be to cultivate greater awareness in daily life.

Return to this practice whenever you remember to throughout the day, even if it is only for five minutes here and there. You can practice mindfulness while on public transport, waiting for an appointment or in conversation with others.

Awareness is also, in a way, "mindlessness". Mindlessness is the intelligence that is present when your mind stops thinking—an intelligence that arises spontaneously. Being totally absorbed in the task at hand will allow your natural awareness to emerge. Give yourself fully to whatever you are doing right now!

NOTICING THE PROCESS

If engaging totally with the present proves difficult, try altering your focus slightly. While you concentrate on being fully aware of whatever is going on, also observe your own reactions. These can be emotions, thoughts or bodily sensations. Just notice all of these factors, and as they come up focus on letting go. If you feel an emotional reaction, recognize it but remind yourself that it is transient. If you feel a stiffness or tension in your body, just notice it, breathe a little more deeply and let the sensation go. If you find your thoughts are going in a certain direction, don't try to pursue them.

LETTING GO

The aim of this practice is to become less reactive to transient thoughts and feelings. You become more aware of impulses or desires to speak and act in a certain way, without necessarily giving in to these impulses. If you find it difficult, you could try silently repeating "let go, let go, let go…" as each response comes up. You may get your first taste of equanimity—not being disturbed by what goes on around you.

PAYING ATTENTION

Bring your focus back to the world around you. Let go of preoccupations with your own reactions and processes. Allow your attention to rest on the objects around you, whether plants or animals, or furniture and other domestic objects. Whenever people approach you, concentrate on paying full attention to them. Acknowledge their presence. Open up to them, focusing on being fully engaged and receptive to their needs. Your innate intelligence will help you with what is needed. As the Buddha said, "How can one ever know anything if they are too busy thinking?"

DIVINE LOVE

Love is the essence of God in every mystical tradition. In Sufism, God is called the Beloved, and Sufi poets, like the fourteenth-century Persian poet Hafiz, used the metaphor of lovers to describe the longing for union with God.

I N TANTRIC TRADITIONS, love unites the feminine principle of energy with the masculine principle of consciousness. This mandala is called the Shri Yantra, and it represents the interpretation of feminine energy (the color red) and masculine energy (white) to depict the necessity for the interplay of both. In the tantric view, the interdependence of opposites, whether feminine or masculine, light or darkness, compassion or wisdom, is fundamental to our existence. An integrated approach to a holistic universe can accept the shadow side of people, and therefore experience and embrace others just as they are. The lotus petals depicted in the two outer circles of the mandala shown here are there to remind us of the transformative power of love.

I sing what I am.
I sing what I love.
I sing because I am loved.
Love sings me
I sing of that love.

I am that love.
I am that.
I am the sound
silence
sings.
—Chloe Goodchild

MEDITATION ON DIVINE LOVE

1 Imagine you are walking through a sunlit glade, deep in a forest. The grass is soft underfoot, and the sun warms your back. Step into the sacred precinct of a temple. You are in a quiet garden with a stream flowing nearby. A soft breeze moves the leaves.

2 A holy image that has meaning and resonance for you will be revealed in this glade. In a shaft of light you see a yogi sitting in contemplation, a halo of light around his or her body; or the Virgin Mary appears from inside the church with her child; or perhaps the Christ figure emerges from behind the tree; or you find a golden egg, a symbol of life. The temple bell rings and you inhale the sweet fragrance of flowers. The sight of this holy figure inspires serenity and calmness. Feel the wisdom and holiness emanating from them, throughout the glade and forest. Feel their wisdom and compassion encompassing you.

3 Experience the consciousness and energy in the created world. Become aware of love as the ultimate nature of reality. The energy of the universe is abundant, warm and nurturing.

4 You might wish to visualize a lotus or rose in your heart. See the flower opening up and blooming. It is nourished by your warm compassion. Let this warmth and tenderness pervade your entire being.

5 If you are finding it hard to conjure the feeling of being bathed in love and expressing love, then imagine a chalice between your breasts. Golden nectar slowly drops into this chalice from the heavens through your crown. Every time you do this meditation, the chalice steadily fills up, until you are so full of love that it overflows. Allow the overflow to reach those around you.

6 Offer your love and gratitude for the created world to the Creator.

The love of the divine is what completes us as human beings, rather than the romantic love that the West idealizes, witnessed in so much of its culture. Tantric sex teaches us the process of bringing the divine back into love, so that love-making becomes a doorway to the sacred. We long to lie in the divine all-encompassing embrace, and Tantra shows a way toward truly divine love through relating with an earthly partner.

THE PATH OF DEVOTION

By constantly affirming love through meditation, you can actualize the power of love. In aligning with love, all that is not love diminishes in your life. The image of love of God or creation is the symbol for the path of devotion. Bhakti yoga describes the Hindu path of devotion, in which you surrender to absorption in the divine—or love.

Traditional guidance from the *Bhagavad Gita* for fostering a sense of complete union suggests meditating and reflecting on the divine, glorifying divine attributes and talking and thinking about the divine. Through worship you offer up prayers and carry out service to others in the name of love. You create an intimate, loving relationship with the divine and dedicate your life to love. You surrender your life up to the divine and thus surrender to love.

A DIVINE IMAGE

You can meditate while gazing at an image or icon, so use whichever image is relevant to you, whether of Buddha, Shiva/Shakti, Jesus, Mary or an enlightened master to help you connect with divinity. Close your eyes and conjure up a divine world inside, or use the mandala we have created to feel centered within a holistic, loving universe.

In using the Shri Yantra for meditation, reflect on the many faces of love. The inter-penetration of five female and four male triangles creates myriad other triangles, which can be seen in meditation as an array of different states of consciousness. Although we often think in terms of polarized opposites, the dynamic interplay of Shiva and Shakti creates qualities such as passion, compassion, inner knowledge, bliss and awareness.

As the Sufi poet Rumi says, "God turns you from one feeling to another and teaches by means of opposites, so that you have two wings to fly, not one."

COMPASSION

This mandala depicts Tara, a goddess believed to have been formed from tears of compassion, regarded by many tantric Buddhists as the saviour of all. Her whole body is made of light and she holds a lotus flower, symbol of regeneration.

COMPASSION IS THE emotion that arises in the heart in response to witnessing the suffering of others. Focusing on the inherent suffering of life allows us to develop a compassionate stance, an actively open and caring orientation toward other people.

Our lives are privileged in comparison with others throughout the world, many of whom live in conditions so challenging that their scant resources can never be enough.

Compassion is that which makes the heart move at the pain of others. It crushes and destroys the pain of others. It is called compassion because it shelters and embraces the distressed.

—The Buddha

MEDITATION ON COMPASSION: LOVING KINDNESS

1 The loving-kindness meditation develops the habit of altruism. It is a heart meditation. Cultivate a helpful attitude at work, in your relationships and with strangers. Maintain a friendly and hospitable attitude toward everybody, regardless of whether you think you like them or not.

2 Develop in yourself an emotion of loving acceptance toward yourself, including those things you don't like—your shadow side. Through self-acceptance you can integrate them into your whole personality. Now feel compassion toward yourself, empathizing with your suffering before dispersing it in the ocean of compassion.

3 Direct this emotion of compassion toward someone you respect: a teacher, mentor, or role model. Now send these sentiments toward those you love, such as your child or partner. Imagine them receiving and being nourished by the energy of your positive intentions.

4 Next, extend this emotional largesse to acquaintances or strangers. If you wish to focus on extending the energy of love that has arisen in you to someone else in need, visualize them enfolded in your heart.

5 Lastly, focus on sending loving acceptance toward someone you are in conflict with. If you can melt your hostile emotions, you can see your enemies as being in as much need of help as the rest of us. Each act of generosity acknowledges our fundamental interdependence. Let love shower them, warming and nurturing them.

Many people alive today are ill, suffering, neglected, exploited, displaced, dispossessed or dying. While it may be distressing to observe others in their pain, the experience can be used to strengthen compassion.

EMPATHY PRODUCES COMPASSION

Appreciate the relative peace and comfort that you live in and the fact that freedom from the struggle for survival allows you to generate your own personal dreams and to pursue them. It has also left you with the emotional capacity to empathize with the sufferings of others, which gives rise to compassion.

Compassion is not pity. It is as pure gold, because it orients you toward others in a receptive, communicative and connected way. When you are feeling friendly, you reach out to include other people. Try to treat them with genuine kindness, warmth and understanding for their foibles. These are merely the idiosyncrasies of character produced by personal reactions to events in their particular life story. Foster an attitude of openness toward others, and listen for the messages behind words and appearances. Send out reciprocal feelings of helpfulness and loving kindness toward those who are open to you. You can extend this empathy practice by radiating loving kindness to all those in need.

START WITH YOURSELF

In Buddhist practice, compassion is the result of love that is generated as you develop your spiritual awareness. Loving yourself is the first step to loving others. Once you are in touch with the compassionate, accepting energy of love, you can love the whole of creation, even those aspects that might not seem obviously lovable. Love is always relational, even when you are focusing on self-love. Loving yourself is loving who you are, just as you are. Then you can love your partner, family, friends, community and God, just as they are.

This loving acceptance is an attitude of divine love, as a creator might feel toward all forms of life, regardless of what form it might take. Accept, embrace and love your own character—even your neuroses.

FORGIVENESS

Lack of forgiveness is one of the most corrosive of negative emotions. Forgiveness is the key to inner peace because it transforms your attitude from fear and blame into love and acceptance. It is not a sign of weakness, but of strength.

LACK OF FORGIVENESS can be a barrier to feeling connected with others. In refusing to forgive past wrongs done to us, we close down our hearts and so end up suffering further. Unfortunately we end up punishing ourselves on top of the trauma we feel that we have already experienced at the hands of others. Refusing to forgive can bind you into a hateful negativity that disturbs your equilibrium.

A NO-WIN SITUATION

The usual reason for holding on to our lack of forgiveness is wanting the other person to acknowledge responsibility for their actions. However, the most common reaction from others is denial, so you find yourself in a no-win situation. In refusing to forgive, you damage yourself further and reduce your capacity for happiness and openness. Spending energy trying to justify your own actions or pinning blame on others keeps you in an antagonistic, blaming mode. The desire of others to wound you—if there is any truth in it—is mirrored by your desire to blame.

In order to let go of past pain, hurt and anger, you can choose to focus on forgiveness. According to the psychologist Chuck Spezzano, forgiveness is a choice you can exercise. If you feel stuck you can ask for grace to free a stuck situation, and free yourself from your reactions. In circumstances in which you find it difficult to let go, don't forget that you can call to a higher power to help you. You do not need restitution to move forward yourself. Instead, use the situation to examine the limits of your capacity to forgive, and to extend or dissolve these limits.

The weak can never forgive.

Forgiveness is the attribute of the strong.

—Mahatma Gandhi

FORGIVING YOURSELF

It is hard to forgive others without first forgiving yourself. You know that you are angry with what they did to you, but you may also unconsciously be angry at what you did to them. In forgiving, you let go of your own harsh, negative, judgmental thoughts and at the same time forgive your vengeful self. This is another way of integrating your own shadow side—your own demons. And treating someone with compassion and forgiveness is more likely to contribute to healing their wounds than maintaining distance.

Since most people misbehave as a result of ignorance or lack of consciousness, your compassion may encourage greater self-awareness on their part. Ideally, forgiveness should flow in both directions. It takes only takes one person to change the dynamic of a relationship—the other will inevitably respond. However, if the relationship is too toxic to continue, forgiveness will help you fully separate.

Forgiveness is not the same as condoning injustice. Arriving at a place of resolution may involve vowing not to let injustice be repeated in the future—for instance, by campaigning to raise awareness around a particular issue.

The image we have chosen for this mandala is the Buddha, sitting in contemplation. His third hand holds a lotus and his fourth, a feather. The lotus grows in dark, muddy ponds, producing a perfect blossom; while the feather is as insubstantial as our soul. After dealing with your demons—lack of forgiveness, intolerance, hatred or desire for revenge—you may feel light as a feather, or experience the equanimity of an aspiring Buddha.

You can visualize this Buddha and other enlightened beings above you, shining their forgiveness and blessings on you, and those you need to forgive. Let the Buddha's love and forgiveness flow through you, and into others.

Meditation on Forgiveness

1 Sit quietly and observe your breathing. When you are ready, let your mind float off into a deep, star-strewn universe.

2 Find yourself entering a dusky room, suspended in space. There is nothing in this room, but it is glowing with light and feels warm and peaceful. On the floor is a large circle of light. Move to the center and feel strengthened by its protecting embrace.

3 Invite into the room a presence, representing the person or situation that you need to forgive. Hold on to your center as this presence takes shape. Leave it outside the circle while you hold firm at the center. Notice that their power over you reduces.

4 Feel your compassion arise as you gaze at this presence, stripped of their power. Find it in your heart to forgive them. Dissolve all your fear and anger in forgiveness. After several minutes, if you wish, you may allow the presence into your circle, without destabilizing your calmness.

5 Offer an object that represents your reconciliation, and if one is offered back receive it gratefully. Stay in your circle as the presence leaves the room, and allow the blessing of forgiveness to wash through you.

6 Feeling light and free of the past, leave the room for your mind's journey home through space.

THE WHEEL OF LIFE

The Wheel of Life, or Wheel of Becoming, known as the Bhavachakra, is a Buddhist representation of samsara, the cycle of birth, life and death, from which we may liberate ourselves through enlightenment.

LIFE IS LIKE a Ferris wheel—at one moment we are euphoric, and the next in the depths of despair. However, trying to avoid pain, seek security and gratification and preserve our personal comfort zone can make us small-minded and dissatisfied. The challenge is to avoid walling ourselves in, remain open to intense experience regardless of whether we have invited it, benefit from our suffering and not be afraid to make big changes in our lives.

Light

Will some day split you open

Even if your life is now a hard cage,

For a divine seed, the crown of destiny,

Is hidden and sown on an ancient, fertile plain

You hold the title to.

—Hafiz

MEDITATION ON THE WHEEL OF LIFE

1 Contemplate this mandala, which depicts Yama the God of Death, holding the Wheel of Life to remind us that our lives are transient. Within the circle, different phases of existence are depicted. In the center are symbols for the three fundamental emotions that Buddhists believe need to be integrated: lust (cockerel), aggression (snake) and ignorance (pig). Rising above such preoccupations is considered the only way to free ourselves from karma and get in touch with the pure energy that underlies the pleasures and tensions of daily life. Instead, the key is to focus on the energy underlying whatever is problematic about your life.

2 Think about what you need to change in your life and habits. If you change this present moment, you create the possibility of changing the rest of your life. If you let go of whatever is holding you back right now, you can let go of habitual ways of living that aren't effective for you, your family or others. Be open to change. Be open to growing. Be open to everything that you have to experience and learn in this life.

3 In Buddhism the task of incarnation is thought to be to help with human suffering, which implies that you already have the resources and abilities to aid others. Think about what those gifts might be. Life involves developing more conscious awareness to help others bear their burdens.

OLD HABITS DIE HARD

Eastern traditions hold that our lives are framed not only by habits and consequences of actions in this lifetime, but also by patterns accumulated over previous lifetimes, and so we need even more conscious effort to change such deeply embedded habits. The doctrine of reincarnation locates each individual in a stream of energy and consciousness going back generations. Although we cannot always see the deeper reasons for the circumstances we find ourselves in, we know that the Wheel of Life may bring us into a very different relationship to these circumstances. Because hardship—or joy—might have something to teach us, our struggles are potentially liberating.

The notion of karma (see page 130) means that we should be mindful of our connections with others and the potential consequences of our own choices, as these will determine where we find ourselves on the next spin of the Wheel. According to the Noble Eightfold Path taught by Buddha, how we live is crucial to overcoming old habits. What's important is to cultivate true wisdom, to live our lives ethically and to discipline our minds. This means paying attention to our core attitudes, as well as the way we speak, what we do for a living. To change damaging patterns of behavior takes effort, awareness and concentration. Avoid careless actions and reactions by taking responsibility for how you conduct yourself and how you interact with others.

THE CIRCLE OF LIFE

If you don't like the concept of karma, instead you could treat the Wheel of Life as a circle of life and work with it to focus on the balance between different aspects of your life. Divide a circle into sections corresponding to your priorities, such as love, parenting, friendships, work, play, spiritual development. Reflect on what you already spend time doing and what you need to expand in order to nourish yourself. Reflect on the relationships between different segments and be creative about how you could connect them into a harmonious whole. Be proactive in making changes to bring more balance into your life.

In the center of this mandala are the three tendencies toward attachment, hatred and delusion, which the Buddha describes as driving the wheel. Around the hub are realms of humans, animals, hungry ghosts (spirits who are still attached to this world) heaven and hell. The wheel provides a map for processing sensory information, feelings and desire, transforming ignorance and developing greater consciousness so that ageing and dying are in fact preparations for rebirth.

WISDOM

Wisdom is not knowledge, but a deeper level of knowing than the intellectual mind can attain. It is the primordial intelligence of life. You are more likely to gain access to this dimension through stillness. Cultivate the habit of being still.

BUDDHISTS BELIEVE THAT the fundamental nature of the mind is stillness. If you allow yourself to become calm and still, your mind will automatically settle down, creating a sense of inner peace and contentment, and your natural wisdom can flourish. Meditation is a way of cultivating stillness, and uncovering your true nature—one of calm equanimity in which the distracted busyness of the mind gradually subsides. As this layer dissolves, you feel much more engaged with life, and you are free to experience what is going on with greater intensity.

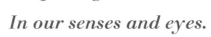

Death is a favor to us,

But our scales have lost their balance.

The impermanence of our body

Should give us great clarity,

Deepening the wonder

In our senses and eyes.

—Hafiz

You can use meditation to curb your mind's endless fantasies or constant analysing of situations, to clear your entanglements with the past and to reduce your worries about the future or about what needs to be done tomorrow. Solutions to problems will become apparent once you are no longer torturing yourself with anxieties, fears, phobias and plans. A state of calmness will allow the mind to drop its habitual concerns and settle into a relaxed acceptance, a vital engagement with being and newness, creating inner peace. As you continue your journey into the deeper spiritual realms, you open to more possibilities and access greater wisdom. Your wisdom is innate.

The *Vijnana Bhairava*, an ancient tantric text, suggests the following techniques (adapted from the translation by Paul Reps):

Wherever your attention alights, experience the attention without attachment. See as if for the first time an ordinary thing, with the consciousness of the god Shiva. Look at the empty space inside the bowl without seeing its walls. Be absorbed into this space, which is existence. Simply by looking steadily at the blue sky beyond the clouds, experience divinity.

Intone a sound, such as A-u-m, so that you slowly hear the sound of existence. Be absorbed in the sound of a stringed instrument, or a song. When eating or drinking, become the taste of food and drink, and savor the joy. Wherever satisfaction is found, enter it deeply, and find bliss.

Put your attention neither on pleasure nor on suffering, but in the place between these. Withdraw your mind from the object of desire and identify with desire. Then you are desire. Feel yourself emanating in all directions, which is your essential self.

Eyes closed, see your inner being in detail. See your nature, which is divine. Place your whole attention on the energy channel, delicate as a lotus stem, in the center of your spinal column. See the lightning-like Kundalini successively piercing each center of energy. In this place, be transformed. Meditate on your body as burning into ashes, and become purified. During sexual union, merge into your beloved, and absorb the divine energy.

According to the Buddha, if we could see the miracle of a single flower clearly, our whole life would change. Tantric wisdom arises through direct experience of the true nature of reality. You can deepen your experience by opening completely toward life and becoming utterly absorbed in objects, experiences and exchanges of energy. Try to stop holding back—it is more important to live intensely and to love wholeheartedly than it is to worry whether you're doing the wrong thing. Trust your inner knowledge.

Instead of rushing to the next thing on your "to do" list, slow down. You will deal with the future when it becomes the present. By cultivating stillness and centeredness, you can begin to trust in your ability to deal with life appropriately. You will know what is needed.

MEDITATION ON WISDOM

1 A good way of cultivating wisdom is to find stillness as much as you can throughout the day. Cultivate the habit of stillness by just stopping and gazing at objects of natural beauty.

2 Really look at a stately tree, appreciating its quality of just being itself.

3 Gaze at a flower, and inhale its scent while being aware of the way it seems to distil its own essence.

4 Gaze at a river or ocean, acknowledging its endless flow, and the cycle of evaporation, cloud formation, rain, in which form is constantly being transmuted.

5 Lose yourself in the spaciousness of the sky, floating like a cloud in its vastness.

6 Allow your identification with nature to generate an intuitive understanding and awareness of your place in nature.

BLISS

Variously described as light, love or vibrant dynamic energy, bliss pervades reality. Spiritual practitioners say that it is ever-present. But to access it, you have to drop your conditioning. Meditation is the key to achieving this.

DELIGHTFUL, INTENSE AND ENVELOPING, bliss is what those who are seeking peak experiences are after—an intense immersion in a fulfilling dynamism. The main obstacle is your own resistance.

In Buddhist practice, meditation is used to let go of a lifelong habit of grasping things, a desire for material goods or a need to control situations. Letting go of your aversion to others or to situations or your craving for reassurance can also be achieved this way. By letting go of your limited perception of life, you open up to a deeper and more satisfying reality.

MEDITATION ON BLISS

1 Relax and deepen your breathing. Imagine your whole body wrapped in a ball of golden light—cocooned in a delicious sensation of bliss. It vibrates through your body, which is humming with delight.

2 Visualize a clear, emerald-green light in the area of your heart. It gradually permeates through your body and expands to color the golden ball emerald green.

3 While floating in the universal heart of the Mother Goddess, focus on the oneness connecting us all. The connection is as light and fine as a web of silk.

4 Experience a deep relaxation and well-being bubbling up in you. Your body vibrates with energy and dances with utter joy. The vibrant well-being that permeates your body is the dynamic energy of the universe.

LOVE

Love brings out the best in everyone and creates more positive energy in the world. Cultivate a loving heart, a loving partnership and a loving home for your family to thrive in. By giving more love, you are more able to receive it.

THE ENERGY OF LOVE is unconditional; an attitude of total acceptance. Love involves a willingness to keep your heart open regardless of whether others behave lovingly toward you. It involves letting go of your expectations of others and allowing them to be themselves. By using meditation to align with love, you are more aware of the love around you; you see the world as a loving place. In the central lotus of this mandala sits a couple in embrace. Start with loving your partner more consciously, and let love radiate from there.

MEDITATION ON LOVE

1 Sit in a lovely, calm place that inspires a softening of your emotional state. Relax your body and breathe deeply and slowly into your belly.

2 Focus your attention in the center of your chest (between your breasts), the heart area.

3 Let go of all thoughts that come in, and become aware of the sensations in this area, whether of joy, sadness, abundance or loneliness, without censoring them.

4 Allow your heart to fill with acceptance and well-being. Use this nourishing energy to soften and melt the sensations in the heart area, whether light or heavy, angry or joyful.

5 As your focus deepens, you may become aware of your heart warming up, or a sensation that it is filling with light or color. Invite this glow to grow within your heart, and let love permeate every aspect of your being and your life.

RELEASE

Your body becomes armoured when you feel tense, anxious or defensive. If you are hard on yourself, you may be critical of others, too. Releasing your body armouring can help you change your habitually harsh attitude to yourself and others.

O NE AIM OF meditation is to learn to give up a lifelong habit of trying to mold situations to suit yourself. This attitude is a real psychological limitation. Learning to let go of manipulation and control can be difficult and painful, however, as it challenges your long-standing self-image. Attempting to control produces physical tension.

This mandala encourages a soft belly, where you release accumulated tension in the lower abdomen. You may follow this meditation with personal power (see page 62) if you then want to build the energy in your hara, or body's power center.

MEDITATION ON RELEASE

1 Relax in a sitting position without drooping, and breathe in and out for some minutes. Slow down your breathing and let each breath sink into your belly, so it rises and falls. Continue until you lose track of time.

2 Draw the air down into your abdomen, and hold your breath. Imagine a ball of light and heat, like a sun sitting in your belly. Let your belly absorb the warmth, softening and relaxing. Encourage the warm rays of the sun to spread through your body and limbs and to diffuse outward, softening your whole being.

3 Let the sun illuminate a shimmering crescent moon, nestling inside the sun and sending a refreshing cool breeze out of your belly. Breathe in this cool breeze and soften your belly as the rays of the sun and moon entwine to fill your being.

LOOKING

Gazing at something is considered in the East to be an active mode of engagement. That is why beauty is so important, as the quality of what you look at can affect your own energy field. You can become totally absorbed in whatever you are viewing.

In India the "third eye", or inner eye, is associated with an energy center (chakra) located on the brow between the two physical eyes. This chakra is considered the seat of the teacher within—your inner knowledge. The third eye responds to the light of wisdom. Regarded as the gateway to inner realms and higher consciousness, it has always been associated with intuition or insight. The third eye is a traditional symbol of wisdom, represented by the dot (bindi) many Hindus wear on the forehead.

Activate your third eye to open you up to imagination, intuition and clairvoyance. Use meditation to break down the barriers between subjective and objective reality. Tantra places great emphasis on throwing yourself into everything that is going on in your life.

MEDITATION ON LOOKING

1 Gaze into the half-lidded eyes of this beautiful mandala. Enter into this gaze, feeling your face become the face you see before you. Look out at the world as a deity might look on creation.

2 Let your awareness pour out through your eyes, into what you are looking at; immerse yourself fully in it. Let all notions of time and space dissolve. Feel yourself lost in a world of indigo vapors. Let the rest of the world drop away and focus on the image. Become the mandala.

3 Feel its eye superimposing itself on your third eye and merging with it.

4 Become that third eye, experiencing the world in the light of your inner wisdom.

LAUGHTER

Laughter makes us feel good, and can be a gift to those around us. Humor and jokes are a vital part of the social glue that binds us together. Emotional expressions of laughter, touch, song, play, tears, and smiles are crucial to well-being and happiness.

THINK FOR A moment how your body feels whenever you laugh or smile. A joyful belly-laugh releases a wave of feel-good endorphins.

In the spirit of Laughing Buddha, Hotei, cultivate these joyful qualities by the practice of laughing. Hotei was a jolly Chinese Zen monk who lived over one thousand years ago, remembered for the ever-replenished sack of goodies he dispensed to all who crossed his path. His pot belly is living proof of his happiness, good luck and plenitude. The Indian teacher Osho conducted "laugh-athons" lasting hours. Since laughing makes us feel so good, we can schedule a session of laughter in order to create the emotions that will carry us through to laughing spontaneously. If you want to remind yourself of something you saw or experienced as side-splittingly funny, you can bring it to mind. Or you can just start to laugh, letting the rhythmically contracting muscles generate more laughter.

MEDITATION ON LAUGHTER

1 Bring to mind something funny that occurred in the past. Generate a laugh.

2 Feel how your face goes into a smile, involving all your features. As you laugh, feel how the laugh arises in your belly, involving your whole torso.

3 Let the laugh take over your whole body. Let it take over your being. You can let the laugh go on for as long as it wants.

4 Let the laughter flow through you. Let yourself become your laughter. Identify with it; let your whole body express it.

DEPRESSION

Depression can result from an accumulation of painful experiences, which ultimately overwhelm you with their negativity, blighting the possibility of interpreting your situation more positively. Use meditation to give yourself a helping hand.

DEPRESSION IS OFTEN the result of layers of deeply compacted pain and sadness, which produce the stark thoughts that you torture yourself with. It can be caused by perceiving yourself as powerless in a situation or feeling victimized by people or events. Instead of hiding behind your hands, let your hands fill with the energy and dynamism that are within you, not far below the surface. This meditation will help you to step out of the prison of depression and into your rightful energy and power.

MEDITATION ON DEPRESSION

1 Do something aerobic for 15 or 20 minutes, and then become still, feeling the energy humming through your body.

2 Immerse yourself in your familiar mood of depression. Experience the weight of it and observe how it saps all your energy. Acknowledge the depth of its darkness. Try to accept the intensity of your feelings without resistance. You may experience hopelessness, loneliness, grief, anger or despair.

3 Can you feel that life is still moving underneath the blanket of depression? Contact the emotions underneath and let them rise to the surface. Emotions are energy. Release the energy held in the depression, letting it surface as howling, anger, raging, terror.

4 Feel how potent you can be when you allow yourself to fill with energy. Affirm your abilities, and positive intentions to transform your life.

PERSONAL POWER

The center of personal power is in the hara, just below the navel. Meditators and martial arts practitioners develop a powerful hara. Use this meditation to generate the energy you need to take your unique place in this world.

WHEN YOU HAVE inner certainty about the way you choose to live your life, you gain power and confidence. Any recognition from others is a bonus, not the reason for seeking empowerment. Your motivation is more to do with expressing the endless reserves you have deep inside. To build the energy that you need to manifest more of your core values, use this meditation to activate your hara, which is like a solar panel or battery that can be charged up. Anything that promotes physical well-being will build up your store of energy here. Our mandala depicts the power-packed potential of the seeds of a sunflower.

MEDITATION ON PERSONAL POWER

1 Stand with your legs firmly planted and take short deep breaths for a few moments, pushing the air out with your abdominal muscles. Feel how your hara is becoming charged up.

2 You can use the image of a sunflower below your navel, or visualize a golden orange-yellow light in your abdomen, glowing with warmth. Imagine this warm glow intensifying into orange and sending a green tendril down into the earth, like the stalk of the sunflower. Or send a tendril of light downward. It will grow into a strong beam of light going straight down and penetrating deep into the core of the earth.

3 With each in-breath, draw energy from the center of the earth up the beam and into your power center. Let this energy renew your strength. Rejoice in feeling strong and potent.

EMOTIONAL DEMONS

Demons have a long history in Hindu and Buddhist mandalas, often depicted haloed in burning flames, or stomped underfoot by enlightened beings. Demons represent our shadow side, which Jung believed was necessary to integrate in order to become whole.

DEMONS ARE ASSOCIATED with ignorance and compulsive negative emotions. When you attempt to drive them away, however, it only seems to give them more power. They are usually figured in mandalas because life encompasses both light and dark. The key to dealing with your personal demons is to get to know them, stripping them of their power over you. They may have something to tell you, because they represent unacknowledged aspects of you that need to be integrated with the self you present to others.

MEDITATION ON EMOTIONAL DEMONS

1 Allow your demon to come into your presence. Notice its shape, its color and its texture. Does it give off a smell, or is there a taste in your mouth as it approaches?

2 Feel your emotional reaction and notice where this is coming from in your body. Accept your reaction. Continue breathing until you feel more comfortable in the proximity of this demon.

3 Invite the demon to settle down in its own place near yours, and center yourself with deep, slow breaths. What are its qualities? If you feel fearful, note what this fear is. Keep breathing.

4 Allow a ring of fire to spring up around you, embracing you in a circle of leaping flames. Imagine that they are destroying your fear, anger and negativity.

5 Feel yourself relax as the flames subside, leaving not dark embers but a softly glowing white light that is almost translucent in quality. Let your fear dissolve and disperse with the particles of light.

DANCE

Like the dancing Shiva in this mandala, your body is a temple, dedicated to the life force. Through it divine energy flows. Let your body express this—dance manifests the dynamic principle of being. Explore it with this meditation, using music if you wish.

F OR MANY OF US, the kinesthetic sense is particularly strong, so the language of movement is one we can easily relate to. Movement is the expression of body knowledge. Devotees of the Hindu god Shiva say that the world was danced into existence. The familiar image of him as the Cosmic Dancer or Lord of the Dance, performing this dance among the flames of the universe, represents the primal creative force. In dance you allow your life force to enliven your body, and encourage your body to express your connection with life. Your dance can be joyful and passionate, or tentative and exploratory. It can be all things depending on where your body and your mood take you.

MEDITATION ON DANCE

1 Stretch your torso, legs, ankles, upper arms and neck, releasing the tension. Stretch your arms and shoulders, circling your shoulders and torso in gentle snakelike movements, and allowing your pelvis to rotate. As you relax your body, allow the energy to calm down. From a place of stillness, let a sense of dynamic energy gather in your body to power your dance.

2 You may wish to dance to some music if you need help to let go. Switch off your brain and allow the dance to find its own rhythm, pace and gestures.

3 Turn off the music if it becomes distracting or restrictive rather than liberating. Let your body dance to the music rather than the music instructing your body. Become the dance.

CONNECTING WITH THE COSMOS

This mandala emphasizes the multiple connections that weave through all life forms. Use the meditation to feel your connection with the cosmos as its energy flows through you and the earth receives your own.

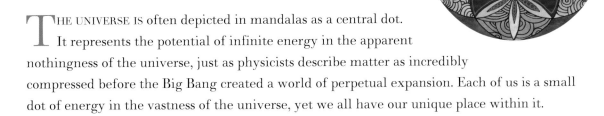

THE UNIVERSE IS often depicted in mandalas as a central dot. It represents the potential of infinite energy in the apparent nothingness of the universe, just as physicists describe matter as incredibly compressed before the Big Bang created a world of perpetual expansion. Each of us is a small dot of energy in the vastness of the universe, yet we all have our unique place within it.

MEDITATION ON CONNECTING WITH THE COSMOS

1 Sit in a comfortable, relaxed, upright position. Breathe gently out, until your lungs are empty. Pause, allow your lungs to fill and then expand them till they are full. Pause, then allow them to empty again. Repeat several times.

2 While breathing out, focus on allowing stuck negative energy in your body to drop down through your abdomen, legs, feet, and then into the earth. With each out-breath, send more stuck negative energy downward in the same way.

3 On each in-breath, begin to draw fresh, pure energy from the core of the earth up to the surface, then into your feet, legs and torso. Allow this energy to go wherever it is needed, to refresh, revitalize and heal you.

4 Imagine you receive pure energy from the cosmos through the crown of your head. Continue to draw energy up from the core of the earth as you breathe in and send negative energy down into the earth as you breathe out.

HEALING

Symptoms are a sign of "dis-ease" or imbalance in the body or psyche. Whatever symptoms you wish to explore, whether pain or unresolved emotional issues, bring them to mind and focus on them. Healing is an infinite resource that anyone can tap into.

ILLNESS IS A SIGN that the body is seeking to readjust after something, such as trauma or neglect, has unbalanced it. Its natural mechanisms tend toward recovery, and we ignore these at our peril, in our ignorance creating the conditions for chronic disease or suffering. Your psyche may be seeking wholeness and purpose, your energy may need rebalancing or your immune system may need support.

MEDITATION ON HEALING

1 Draw in white light through the crown of your head, allowing it to pour over your body and down your legs. Let the light wash through every part of you.

2 When you sense it has covered your whole body, direct the light to where it is needed. Any part of you that feels weak, depleted, blocked or irritated can be cleansed and energized. Let go of pain and suffering. Let go of whatever it is that is stopping you from being whole. Open yourself to the possibility of freedom.

3 Feel the white light revitalize you. See it penetrate your structure like a healing X-ray or ultrasound wave. Let go of darkness. Let healing light cleanse you deeply, on a cellular level.

4 In your mind's eye, visualize your body healed. Feel it lighten. Let the energy flow without hindrance, connecting organs and energy centers with one another. Each part of your body is now in constant communication, sending out pulses of energy and vitality.

WATER

Water is associated with cleansing, the flow of our emotions and the unconscious. We can swim with the currents of our inner life without needing to identify with particular emotions, which are forever changing, like all of life.

EMOTIONS ARE PART of your inner life, and many people feel they have responses to life that are as deep as the ocean. Rather like a surfer on the crest of a wave, the trick is to enjoy the thrill of feeling emotions, without getting sucked under through identifying with a particular emotion. Whether it is pride or envy, anger or sadness, malice or martyrdom, none of them defines our true nature.

Use this meditation to wash away intense emotions. You may want to sit where you can hear the gentle sound of running water.

MEDITATION ON WATER

1 As you breathe in through your nose, connect with the divine source and feel a flow of water descending. Feel yourself rushing up toward the divine source. As you breathe out through your mouth, visualize yourself sitting in a waterfall.

2 Focus on the quality of water. You are as perfect as a single drop, connected to every other drop of water. Breathe deeply and let go into your element of flow.

3 Like a fish gliding through moving water, go with the flow of emotional currents, moving easily around obstacles. Relax in the water, no matter how turbulent it is.

4 Come up from the water into a fine drizzle of warm rain. Let the rain wash any clinging emotions from you as you step into the light—calm, poised and cleansed.

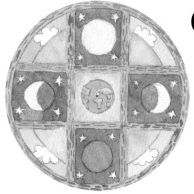

GRATITUDE

In this meditation you celebrate being alive. There are so many good aspects to your life—try to give thanks for them every day. Start by making a list, and then go through the list calling up and experiencing your appreciation.

THE THINGS YOU give thanks for will depend on you and your life but you could start with your very existence, your energy, vitality and health. They will also almost certainly include your home, food and money, and the important people in your life, such as your family, friends and community, and all those people who have been instrumental in making you the person you are.

You'll also feel gratitude for your natural talents, the skills you have acquired and the ways you have overcome obstacles and turned dark moments into something constructive. Don't forget to give thanks for the things you have created, what you have taught others and the numerous ways you have cared for people and they for you.

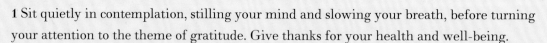

MEDITATION ON GRATITUDE

1 Sit quietly in contemplation, stilling your mind and slowing your breath, before turning your attention to the theme of gratitude. Give thanks for your health and well-being.

2 Turn your attention to the mentors and teachers who have inspired you, the companions you have found along the path and the relationships you have—for the opportunity to love with a warm heart.

3 Appreciate your personal abilities, and celebrate your accomplishments and successes.

4 End by focusing on possibilities for growth and change, or invite into your life qualities that you feel you need.

DEITY PRACTICE

This is a lovely meditation in which you can use the image of a deity figure such as a god, an angel or a saintly figure to evoke divine qualities, which you can then generate in yourself. We are all sacred manifestations of the divine.

BRING TO MIND the qualities you would like to cultivate. Think about your strengths and also your limitations. How would you like to grow and develop so that your weaknesses are less limiting? Reflect on what attracts you to spiritual figures and practices. Which qualities provide a positive role model? Perhaps you'd like to be more loving, calm and wise, dynamic and comfortable with your body, or knowledgeable and thoughtful so that when you speak it is something worth contributing.

MEDITATION ON DEITY PRACTICE

1 Gaze at this mandala, or an object that is symbolic of the qualities you wish to cultivate, or call a picture into your inner eye. Whether your idea of the divine is represented by a snake, a golden egg, the Buddha or the Virgin Mary, imagine this deity appearing before you.

2 Feel the energy of their presence coming toward you and enveloping you like a cocoon. Let their loving compassion, their wisdom and mercy, their serenity or dynamism permeate your own being. Imagine that this energy is incorporated into your own being, pervading your mind, and then your heart and your whole body.

3 Become that deity. Feel your own dynamism and compassion, your own love and wisdom. Feel these qualities emanating now from your own radiant being. Dwell in the experience of a divine being who has realized full potential.

BEING OF SERVICE

Learning to put someone else's needs before your own can be a real lesson in spiritual growth. That's why your children are often your best teachers—their demands won't allow you to disengage with life or focus too much on your problems.

EACH ACT OF giving or caring affirms our interdependence. Rather than focusing on what you imagine you need, focus on what you have to offer others. How can you give something that will benefit others? Do you have spare time to offer support, companionship and practical help? Can you tune into someone else's reality and imagine what they might need? Can you bear the neediness, pain or longings of someone else? Can you just be present and witness the struggles of others without backing off?

The following meditation can happen at the bedside of someone ill, or you can hold someone's favorite possession or a photo to help you tune into their needs.

MEDITATION ON BEING OF SERVICE

1 If you are sitting next to the person, let your breathing fall into the same rhythm as theirs. If you are holding an object instead, concentrate on the person it represents, allowing their essence to enter your own being through your breath.

2 Focus on how they must be feeling. Try to feel how they experience their body: relaxed or uncomfortable and irritated?

3 Focus on their emotional state. How is their mood? How do they experience their life and its burdens?

4 Consider what would be helpful to them, emotionally or practically. By "tuning in' for some time, you may be able to come up intuitively with something useful. Check later as to whether they would prefer some other form of help.

PASSION

Kundalini is a libidinal energy that we might describe as lust for life. Traditionally it is represented by a snake goddess, coiled asleep around the base chakra, or energy center, at the bottom of your spine. Awakening it awakens your passion and energy.

THE ENERGY OF the base chakra is represented by fire, which is often evoked in meditations. Just as sacrificial fires are used to reduce substances to their essence—in the form of ash—so fire visualizations like this one can purify your desire and transform it into commitment. With this meditation, you will emerge from the ashes purified, with new energy. Experience your inner fire as a wholehearted aliveness. Allow it to become a dynamic force motivating your every thought and action.

MEDITATION ON PASSION

1 Use the image of fire for this meditation, and imagine awakening the sparks of life at the base of your abdomen. Allow the hot embers to warm your abdomen.

2 Lie down and relax deeply. As you inhale, imagine you are drawing energy up your legs from your feet and into your sexual energy center, in the lower pelvis. Visualize this breath as a deep, blood-red color.

3 Hold your breath a moment, allowing the vibrant red light to warm your pelvis. As you exhale, encourage it to saturate your pelvis in its warm red glow. Imagine it invigorating your entire body.

4 Each time you breathe in, allow your whole being to become imbued with this energy, the powerhouse of your lust for life.

5 Each time you breathe out, imagine this life-affirming passion embracing your whole life. Allow it slowly to consume your body as flames. From the ashes, step forth with new commitment to your life.

CHAKRA

Chakra techniques teach us how to purify and invigorate Kundalini, the energy center at the bottom of the spine, at the base chakra. The purpose of raising Kundalini energy is enlightenment, when you become fully integrated.

THERE ARE SEVEN PRINCIPAL chakra points along the spine, and hundreds of minor ones, constituting a network of subtle energy channels. Energizing the chakras is believed to help the Kundalini on its journey from the base of the spine up toward the crown of the head.

MEDITATION ON CHAKRA

1 Lie on your back and breathe deeply and slowly. With every in-breath, concentrate on the energy gathering around the base chakra. Imagine the energy as a warm red glow.

2 Breathe in and feel the energy quicken and climb upward, into the second chakra, at your navel. Focus on the orange glow of energy in your belly.

3 Draw up the energy on your in-breath till you feel a bright yellow energy emanating from your solar plexus, under where the ribs meet.

4 Breathe the energy into your heart area. Become aware of an intense green glow there, pulsating with love.

5 Breathe into your throat area, until you feel a deep blue energy full of everything you want to express.

6 Breathe in the energy up to your third eye. See a violet light arising from the clarity of your vision.

7 Draw the energy up to your vertex, where the pulsating white light of a thousand-petalled lotus links your energy body with the energy of the universe.

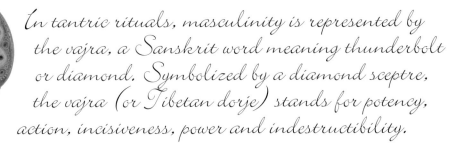

MASCULINITY

In tantric rituals, masculinity is represented by the vajra, a Sanskrit word meaning thunderbolt or diamond. Symbolized by a diamond sceptre, the vajra (or Tibetan dorje) stands for potency, action, incisiveness, power and indestructibility.

THE VAJRA WAS WIELDED by Indra, who in Vedic times was the supreme ruler of the Hindu gods, the god of war and storms and the greatest of all warriors. Among the classic masculine archetypes of the king, the warrior and the magician-healer, the true warrior sums up a situation and takes direct action to bring positive change. Although he is powerful, he acts wisely and takes care not to harm others. Aggression, the typical attribute of an immature masculinity, is repulsive to the warrior. The hardest thing the warrior does is to look directly at his own attitudes, expose their limitations and then step beyond them.

MEDITATION FOR MASCULINE CONSCIOUSNESS

1 To develop clarity and stillness, imagine yourself holding the diamond vajra, or sceptre. You can see deeply, and understand deeply. With your knowledge comes calm. You are already in control, but there is no need to impose control.

2 Feel your power arise, and practice containing it within your stillness. It is a means of coming to a plan of action or developing a strategy rather than a knee-jerk response.

3 Affirm that you are always able to develop a thought-out strategy whose aim is to access the truth; imagine yourself as a spiritual seeker. Invite the truth to flow into you.

4 Appreciate all the wisdom you have accumulated in your bones. Feel how this connection gives you inner strength and allows you to be strong, quietly radiating your own sense of self-mastery and competence.

FEMININITY

Femininity is divine, and manifests the qualities of the Goddess, or the Great Mother. In the East, the feminine is passionate, earthy, powerful, expressive, open, giving, caring, sharing. She is all-powerful, all-seeing and all-merciful.

THE HINDU goddess Shakti is associated with dynamic energy. Masculinity is associated with consciousness, and in a holistic universe both are needed to manifest life. Eastern traditions have always regarded women as sexually dynamic, and initiators of men. This role was once enshrined in temple dancers. In Greek and Roman mythology, the goddess Artemis/Diana, the huntress, represented the go-getting aspect of women. In Delphi, the priestess Pythia had a sacred role as the transmitter of the oracle messages from the gods.

MEDITATION ON FEMININITY

1 Reflect on ancient goddesses and their qualities: energy, dynamism, passion, power, awareness, intuition, care, concern, nurturance. You are a queen. Your nature is one of innate power.

2 Imagine you are sitting on your throne, emanating power. You have much to share that you can bestow on others. See the subjects you love and care for as they come to you for help. You can communicate easily, sharing your wisdom and insights with others. Your intuitive faculties are awake and picking up information about the situations and responses of others. You can empathize, without loss of your own sense of self, knowing that you do not have to give your power away.

3 Your beauty is internal—your essence pours out of you. You have no inhibitions in manifesting the potency of your being.

4 As much as you give you receive. Love is there all around you, flowing through you. Flowing into you. Flowing out.

SEXUALITY

Tantric practitioners have long known that sex can be a gateway to ecstatic experience, extending your awareness of bliss. Deepening the sexual energy between you and your beloved means connecting to the primal erotic energy of creation.

THE MARRIAGE of man and woman is represented within tantra by the image of the god Shiva and his consort, Shakti, in sexual union. The fruits of their divine connection rain down upon the world as nectar. Cultivating this sacred model in your own love-making aligns you with the perfect god and goddess. One practice in tantric meditation is to visualize Shakti and Shiva making love above the crown of your head. The golden nectar rains down into a winged chalice positioned where your third eye would be.

The following meditation presents the world as conceived by love and sustained by love. Just as you were conceived and brought into this world as a result of your parents' sexual love, so was the whole world.

MEDITATION ON SEXUALITY

1 Make love as though the love that you are making is sacred, and as if you are both divine. Your partner is your cherished Beloved.

2 On reaching orgasm, meditate on the bliss that expands from your joined genitals, seeing it as waves of energy running though your body, nourishing you both and your families, and then radiating through the whole world.

3 In your post-coital bliss, experience the whole of creation as sexual in nature. Feel at one with creation and know that you are the source of it. Let sexual energy flood your mind and body in ecstatic waves.

CONCEPTION

According to tantric philosophy, conception occurs when the lovers' energy bodies are revitalized by the energy of sexual ecstasy. A vortex of swirling energy rises up through the crown of the head and attracts a soul that is already waiting to be reborn.

SEXUAL BLISS constitutes semen, which is mixed with the secretions created through the woman's bliss. The ovum is thus fertilized in the consciousness of bliss, which attracts all that the new life will need. Your mental state during love-making is important and is believed to determine some of the attributes of the coming baby or the experiences of family life. Making love in joy provides a harmonious container for family life.

MEDITATION ON CONCEPTION

1 To optimize conception, make love consciously, visualizing yourselves as two divine creatures in union, so your mental state is conducive to perfect harmony.

2 A natural closeness after sexual orgasm deepens the bonding process. Leave your genitals joined together after intercourse so that your love juices are mixed and your individual energies are exchanged. (Taoists believe that this will have a revitalizing effect on both of you and will nourish you psychically.)

3 Focus on your belief that you can provide the environment that this new life needs, whatever the imperfections of your life and character. Feel confident that your circumstances and personalities will provide the crucible for relevant life lessons that this new soul has come to learn.

4 Feel secure that any new life that comes from your sexual union is coming because on some level it has chosen to do so—and that therefore it is all right, whatever your situation is.

RELATIONSHIP

What is key to reciprocity and connection is allowing the "otherness" of the other. Let them be themselves without trying to change them. Express love through tenderness, caring and compassion, and nurture the sexual side of your relationship.

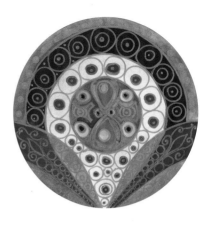

IN THIS EXERCISE, you meditate in the space after orgasm, with one partner acting as a guide or witness for the other. Regular meditations with your partner will nourish your relationship and create a firm bond between you, strengthening your closeness. During sex you may have approached an altered state, and meditating afterwards will consolidate and expand that experience. This mandala has two interlocking infinity symbols.

MEDITATION ON RELATIONSHIP

1 Allow yourself to fall into a state of deep relaxation. Your partner can speak to you just sufficiently to stop you from dropping off to sleep, by prompting you to describe your state. Lie together, focusing on harmonizing your energy bodies, or lie together with your heart wide open, full of love for your partner.

2 Observe any associations, sensations, emotions, images or fantasies that arise as you enter this state of meditation. Allow them to arise spontaneously.

3 Describe them to your partner, who should listen without comment or interpretation, acting as a witness. The process of finding words to express your experience and share it with your partner connects you consciously, as well as the energy connection you have already created during this meditation.

4 Now listen to your partner as they describe the experience to you. Continue to maintain the atmosphere of receptivity and loving attentiveness.

GUILT

We have all made mistakes, but what matters is whether we learn from them. We need to be compassionate and forgiving toward ourselves, as well as others. Our mistakes arise from lack of awareness or consideration.

Guilt is anger turned inside yourself, stemming from your conscience's views of what is right and wrong. If you have learned to act with integrity, you can let go of your self-hatred. You have made a commitment not to behave in that way again, so you can forgive yourself for your past misdeeds. Learn tolerance toward yourself and others, as well as respect. You can use this meditation to go through a list of regrets from the past, healing your guilt, shame or embarrassment with self-forgiveness.

MEDITATION ON GUILT

1 Take responsibility for your actions, being aware of possible consequences and being mindful of the needs and rights of others. Treat others with the respect with which you would like to be treated. Forgive yourself for lapses of awareness and treat them as opportunities for growth and to become more aware.

2 Cultivate positive attitudes. Steer your mind toward love for other forms of life—we are all connected.

3 Evoke feelings of understanding and compassion for the multiple mistakes that humans make, owing to lack of awareness or a desire for short-term gains. We all make mistakes. Summon up an attitude of forgiveness.

4 Now recall each incident you wish to heal, and dissolve it in the well of compassionate understanding, self-acceptance and forgiveness that has arisen in your heart.

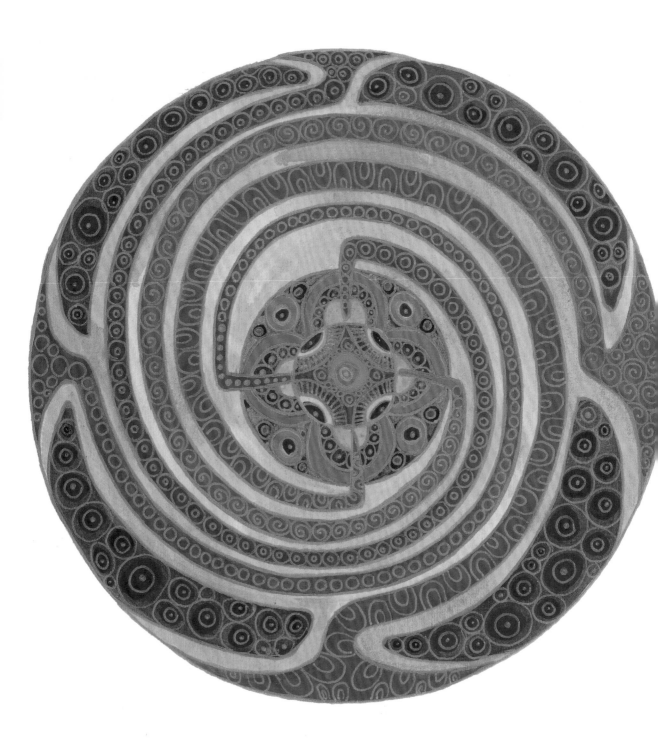

SUCCESS

Success is about expressing your personality and vision of the world and following your own path in life. Few of us believe we are total successes or total failures. Learn to transform any doubts about yourself into a belief in your ultimate success.

ALL SUCCESS is relative—one moment you are in demand, and the next you're out of favor. A fear of failure can make us sabotage the good things that come into our lives, give up far too easily or not even try in the first place. We may also fear success, suspecting that if we're successful, fate will knock us down—or others will no longer like us, through envy or competitiveness. But if you have an open, positive attitude and show you are interested in people, they will feel your empathy and be receptive to you. Let the world work with you. Throw yourself into whatever you are passionate about. What you set your heart on is what you become. Allow yourself to take more space in the world.

MEDITATION ON SUCCESS

1 Visualize your fear and limitations as a stagnant flow of energy that needs to be moved. Take several long, slow breaths, imagining that your breath is loosening this energy and getting it to flow. As you breathe out, release the fear—more with each out-breath.

2 Feel a ball of quiet confidence growing in your solar plexus. With each in-breath send more energy to this area.

3 Encourage this golden ball to expand, bringing an increased sense of well-being and a knowledge that you are likeable and successful. Feel an inner power and a quiet certainty about your worth.

4 Feel your confidence expanding through your being. Recognize that you have all the energy you need but that fulfilling your sense of purpose will give you even more. Let yourself shine.

ABUNDANCE

The cornucopia is an ancient symbol of plenty: a horn of fruits, sea creatures and shells, representing the abundance of nature. This mandala is about recognizing the abundance that is all around us—and seeing that we are all part of the profusion of life.

To DISCOVER YOUR own abundance, it is important to recognize your personal talents, accomplishments and successes—all the good things you are manifesting now. You are more abundant than you recognize. Concentrate on what it is that you need for your life to be more fulfilled. Invite the seeds of those qualities to come into your own life. Prepare the soil, then relax. Allow abundance to flow into you and all around you.

MEDITATION ON ABUNDANCE

1 You may find it useful to do this meditation in nature. Gather items that represent nature, such as crystals, water, a feather, a candle, incense.

2 Contemplate the cup of abundance. Visualize the horn-shaped cornucopia, or a chalice, which gradually fills up.

3 Observe how full it is. Then notice that it is being replenished. Let it fill, so it reaches the brim. It becomes so full that it begins to overflow. Enjoy the profusion of water as it pours over the side of the cup.

4 Visualize yourself diving into the cup and immerse yourself fully in this quality of abundance.

5 When you have sufficiently enjoyed the cup and experienced its blessings, let go of the need for a container and allow yourself to join the overflow—without worrying where it will take you.

6 You may wish to explore the possible directions in which the overflow may take you, and visualize what unexpected gifts will be brought to you.

SELF-ESTEEM

Your deeper nature is passionately engaged with life, even if you come across as shy and hesitant, but low self-esteem can hold you back and cause you to cut yourself off from others. Learn to value your own nature and make the most of your sensitivity.

SELF-DOUBT AND INSECURITY obscure your awareness of your own personal power. Guilt, shame, self-hate or fear can get in the way of engaging with life. Other signs of low self-esteem include settling for less because you think you don't deserve better, or simply being confused about what you want. Clinging to the past and dysfunctional attachments to people or situations will get you nowhere. Instead, recognize your sensitivity as an asset, which keeps you in touch with your emotions and also with the vulnerabilities of others.

MEDITATION ON SELF-ESTEEM

1 Can you recognize yourself in this circle of vibrant women? Acknowledge that you are a shining being—as valued and as worthy as any other. Accept that you connect with others in subtle ways—through intuition and sensation. Because your awareness is primed, you are able to reflect on what is going on in certain situations.

2 Realize that nature has its own value, and appreciate it, even when it makes you insecure or socially awkward. Value and nurture your own character, to provide your own security. This will help you heal earlier experiences that have leached away your confidence.

3 As you gain confidence, learn to stand in your own personal power and be seen as who you are. Be prepared to expose yourself, in all your sensitivity as well as your strengths.

CHILDHOOD

To become more integrated and mature, many of us need to heal experiences from early childhood, turning them into lasting, character-building assets. This meditation will help you consider how your personal qualities have made you who you are.

GAZE AT THE MANDALA to evoke some happy experiences of childhood. Look at photographs of yourself as a child, to help you feel your way back into your childhood experiences. How would you describe your personal qualities then? What were your strengths and weaknesses? How were these aspects of you received? Did your parents appreciate you or did they try to make you change? Reflect on how you developed and worked on these qualities. How did the qualities that made life difficult as a child help you in your current life?

MEDITATION ON CHILDHOOD

1 Focus on the positive attributes of yourself as a child. Feel the emotions you experienced whenever your way of engaging in the world was fruitful. Let your early qualities of sensitivity, shyness, perseverance, anger, strength or playfulness wash over and energize you.

2 Recognize that those childhood qualities are still there, and allow them to nourish and support you.

3 Welcome the healed child. Embrace the loved child. Play with the playful child. Acknowledge the wise, all-knowing child.

4 Integrate the child who has always been present with your own true self, your own essence.

5 Rejoice that you, this integrated personality, have grown into someone who is actualizing their potential.

SUFFERING

Suffering offers the possibility of spiritual redemption, if you can find the resources inside yourself to transform your trials into growth. Spiritual practice involves asking yourself what lessons you need to learn for positive change.

SUFFERING CAN BE the result of physical dysfunction or emotional pain. Physical pain demands surrender, but many of us hold on to our emotional pain. In very challenging or dark moments, opportunities for growth exist—indeed, without difficulty and challenges, it can be hard to sustain the effort needed to grow. Through them you can develop qualities you might not otherwise have, benefiting yourself and others.

MEDITATION ON SUFFERING

1 The Buddhist practice of tonglen (giving and receiving) is an extraordinary meditation connected with utilising your struggles with negativity and suffering to benefit others and at the same time overcome a fear of suffering. On the in-breath, you open to all the suffering that is an inevitable part of the human condition, while on the out-breath you radiate all that is great about being alive.

2 Remain open with every in-breath, inhaling the suffering all around. Not only do you invite in all your own unresolved issues, your doubts and pain, but you invite in those of others. Draw in all the suffering of others, in whatever form it takes. Take it on yourself in order to spare them their suffering. Know that you are strong enough to bear it.

3 Breathe out joy. Breathe out strength, competence, calmness, solidity, awareness, happiness, fearlessness, bliss. The world needs these qualities and you are able to share them.

THE TREE OF LIFE

Trees shade us and nourish us. They are the lungs of the earth. With their immense fertility and longevity, they are universal sources of inspiration, and the Tree of Life has been a potent symbol in every ancient culture.

THE TREE OF LIFE often symbolizes the uniting of heaven and earth; birth, maturity, death and rebirth; or man's place in the universe. Man can be seen as one of the fruits of the tree, and in some esoteric traditions the tree provides a "map of creation". It can also be seen as a symbol of the collective because it represents community—an example of companionship and exchange.

MEDITATION ON THE TREE OF LIFE

1 Visualize yourself sitting in the shade of an ancient, majestic tree. Its heavy boughs and leafy branches describe an imperfect sphere. Its trunk is solid, gnarled and wrinkled, supporting younger and younger branches, tipped with vivid new shoots. Water and nutrients are being pumped throughout the abundant growth.

2 The tree supports a myriad of wildlife. Birds nest there, and small animals and insects have made their homes in nooks and crannies.

3 This tree has weathered severe storms, unstable weather and the depredations of pollution and mankind, from children climbing it to adults seeking firewood. Yet it is still standing and offering support and protection to all who come near.

4 In the shadow of this tree, a group of students are discussing life. Sit in the shade of this awesome tree and listen to the murmur of voices and signs of life. Experience how protected and supported you are by this glorious tree.

EARTH

This meditation is for you if you live more in your head than your heart or body, as it will help you to feel grounded. Many of us feel ungrounded—we are driven by hectic lifestyles and are forced to communicate though depersonalizing modern technology.

BEING GROUNDED MEANS inhabiting your body; and experiencing your body as supported by nature. Use the mandala to feel even more physically and emotionally nourished by nature. If the weather is good you could perform the meditation outdoors, so that you can use the sounds, smells and other sensations of nature as stimuli in your visualization. You don't actually have to be in a beautiful place, because your imagination can summon it up.

MEDITATION ON EARTH

1 Take off your shoes and find a tranquil spot in your garden or on a balcony. Failing that, gaze at a plant or flower, or call up an image of nature, such as a wild piece of coast or a sacred grove.

2 Be aware of the textures, smells and sounds, allowing all these sensory impressions to penetrate your body. You can feel the hardness of the earth underfoot, hear the birds, smell the scents wafting on the breeze and feel it against your skin.

3 Rest in the energy of this place. Let it sustain you. Absorb the rays of the sun. Like a plant, suck up any moisture—you are part of the web of life.

4 Now imagine standing on a globe. Through the soles of your feet, sense the energy of the molten lava at the earth's core, turbulent, boiling, beneath the apparent solidity of the earth's crust which is supporting you. It's an aspect of your own being. Sense the vital power that you have deep within yourself.

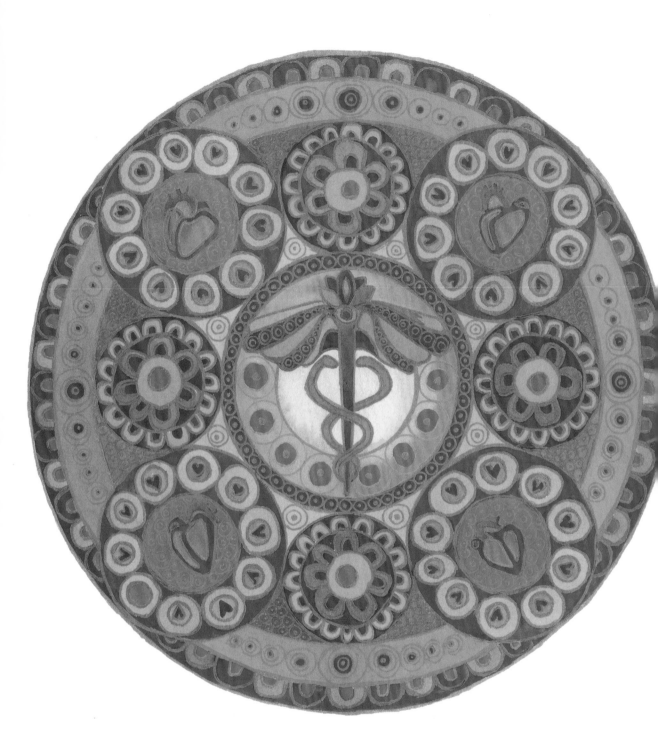

PAIN

Pain can feel like a tormenting demon that cuts right into you. Severe pain goes to your very essence. People who have learned pain management strategies say that ultimately you have to surrender to it, rather than trying to fight it.

FINDING A GAP between bouts of pain might provide a moment's respite in which to find a new way of dealing with it. Pain causes anxiety, which lowers the pain threshold, but the calm relaxation this meditation induces helps break that vicious circle by reducing the anxiety. Although it will not eliminate the pain, it may help you cope with it better.

MEDITATION ON PAIN

1 Rest on the bed, trying to feel relaxed. Allow the floor or bed to take your full weight, so that you feel supported. Become aware of your whole body, feeling it as one, undivided by your experience of pain.

2 Take a deep breath and let the breath snake down through your vital organs, like a golden healing light that brings nourishment and healing energy. Breathe this golden light into your throat, down through your lungs, around the heart, through your diaphragm and into your stomach, liver, gall bladder, pancreas, spleen and intestines. Breathe the healing golden light into your bladder and genitals, your uterus or testicles. Let the breath carry the healing energy through all parts of your body.

3 Now call the pain forth again, but this time accept it, so that the edges of the sensation blur. As you breathe in, breathe into the pain. As you breathe out, release pain. Allow the gap between the in-breath and the out-breath to lengthen, and in that gap release the pain.

FLOW

"Flow" is a state of heightened experience that athletes, artists and musicians may have when they are completely absorbed in expressing their creativity authentically. Being authentic involves being true to your vision and doing whatever it is that needs to be expressed.

FOR SOME THIS creativity could be expressed through playing a musical instrument; for others it could be through teaching, gardening, writing, singing, parenting or meditating. It doesn't matter whether others see it as worthwhile—this is about what you want to express. The golden rule for entering your flow is to follow your heart's desire.

MEDITATION ON FLOW

1 Gaze at the mandala and evoke times when you have been in your flow. Think about whether you spend enough time "in your passion"—doing whatever it is that you feel so passionate about.

2 Do you *know* what you feel passionate about? Consider whether you have yearnings or dreams that you have never had time to explore. What are the things in life that really make you feel excited, energized, engaged… as if you might be making a difference?

3 Sit and reflect on those pursuits that give you most energy and stimulate your vitality. What awakens your senses or makes your heart sing? What satisfies your soul? Which activities or states do you feel really express your core principles or your deepest essence?

4 Spend some time getting in touch with the bodily experiences you have undergone when you have felt most passionate about life. Let the energy of your passion fill your abdomen. Take deep breaths into your abdomen.

5 Fill your abdomen with your desire for life—a desire to express your energy and passion and your pure essence.

BOREDOM

Do you dare to taste your own experience and feel your power? To be free and happy, you may have to sacrifice boredom, a sign of disengagement with life. Turn your attention inward and learn to be still, to regain your inner dynamism.

BOREDOM—a perceived lack of external stimulation—is a restless craving for distraction. We use it to cushion ourselves from painful emotions or feelings of emptiness. To replace the discomfort with more pleasant sensations, we become reliant on stimulants like sugar, chocolate, cigarettes, alcohol, drugs or medications. Boredom indicates we have lost interest in the richness of life. The way through it is to let go of your tension and agitation, inhabit your life fully and find your inner resources. Go inside yourself, because what you'll find there is intrinsically interesting.

MEDITATION ON BOREDOM

1 Take several moments to breathe deeply and quieten yourself. Find your own essence inside yourself: a spark of light, a quickening of energy, a core of self-belief, a knowledge of who you are.

2 Allow the light to radiate outward, the energy to flow through your body, your core of faith to expand, your sense of self to become clearer.

3 Let these qualities become even stronger so that you feel solid and secure in yourself. Feel sufficient in yourself, but also abundant.

4 Enjoy being who you are. Appreciate yourself. Allow yourself to be seen, to be visible. Let this energy nourish and energize you. Feel yourself becoming more dynamic, as you feel more satisfied.

CREATIVITY

Your passport to creativity is passion—applying your energy to doing whatever moves you deeply. The closer you are to your own sources of inspiration, the more you will want to manifest that energy, and to share it with others.

KEEP IN TOUCH with your sources of inspiration to provide a direct channel to creative energy. You can be creative in your style of living or you can give birth to ideas, projects or things of beauty or meaning. That includes your children! The most important aspect of creativity is enjoyment—we are all born with whatever produces the creativity, but it can be knocked out of us by the relentless social pressure to conform. You know the process that stimulates creativity, so you know what you need to do to put yourself there.

MEDITATION ON CREATIVITY

1 Call your creativity forth by tempting it with a conducive environment. If esthetics affect your mood, create what you need, whether it is a tranquil, beautiful environment or a lively, noisy, stimulating one.

2 You may need to turn off the controlling part of your brain. Creativity often comes when it's not expected, such as in dreams or while swimming or walking.

3 Open yourself to channeling your abundant creative energy. There is something inside that you feel called upon to express. Harness that restless driving force into an appropriate channel of expression.

4 When this energy is high, it feels as if invention or original thought flows through you, as though coming from a transpersonal realm.

PLANTING THE SEED

This meditation uses the garden as a metaphor for planting seeds in your life and then nurturing the plants. Be clear in your mind what result you are looking for—the kernel containing the potential of what you desire—as you will get what you invoke.

ONCE YOU HAVE established your goal, convert all the potential energy of your intention into the seed of a plant you wish to grow and eventually harvest. Spend several minutes reflecting on the different aspects of the harvest that you wish to reap, then reflect on the appropriate seed of this harvest, until you have a clear image of the kernel.

MEDITATION ON PLANTING THE SEED

1 Focus on preparing the ground in your psyche. Imagine that you are turning it over, feeding it with the necessary compost, so that it is receptive to the seed you wish to plant. Contemplate what you are about to do—visualize turning the earth, with its rich, dark color and heavy, moist odours.

2 When the earth is ready, plant the seed. In your mind's eye, see yourself watering it and nurturing it. Imagine yourself looking after the seedling, ensuring that weeds don't take over. Reflect for a moment on what needs to be done to care for this plant as it is taking hold, drawing goodness into itself and becoming healthy and vital.

3 This represents your own strength and the vitality of your ideas manifesting as they grow, so spend some time reflecting on what you may need to do in order to bring this into actuality. Imagine yourself collecting the harvest, and be open to what this harvest might be. Experience the joy of accomplishment and celebrate what has been achieved.

INVOCATION

Physicists can detect sound waves from the universe. To us, they are only perceptible when you turn your attention away from the incessant noise of the world around you. You can tune into this inner sound—the sound of creation—through reciting "Aum".

THE SANSKRIT WORD AUM has often been used to attune the individual with this cosmic hum. Reciting a mantra focuses your mind on the inspirational energy of sound, filling you with its power. Aum, which Yogis believe is the primal sound of the universe, stands for the supreme reality. It represents what lies behind the past, present and future. According to the Mandukya Upanishad:

A stands for waking life and the mastery of the senses.

U stands for dream states, in which you can access inner wisdom.

M corresponds to silence, in which you still the mind to uncover your true nature.

AUM stands for the totality of life. It is a symbol of everlasting joy.

MEDITATION ON INVOCATION

1 You can use the sound of your voice to sing the sound of peace and silence.

2 Feel a hum or sound rising from your belly, vibrating through your chest and up into your throat, forming the word Aum. Let your mouth form the syllables slowly.

3 Let your love warm your voice and give expression to your inner voice. Let it communicate your longing, your happiness or your connection with the universe. Your energy is aligned to that of the cosmos, through the spiritual power of Aum.

GRACE

*Allow the sacred to touch your life, the way
a shaft of light breaks through the clouds
or filters through a stained glass window.
In Hinduism, the path of grace is from the
universe, through the central energy channel
of the body, the sushumna ("the most gracious").*

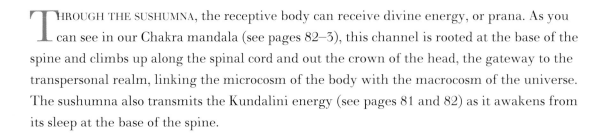

THROUGH THE SUSHUMNA, the receptive body can receive divine energy, or prana. As you can see in our Chakra mandala (see pages 82–3), this channel is rooted at the base of the spine and climbs up along the spinal cord and out the crown of the head, the gateway to the transpersonal realm, linking the microcosm of the body with the macrocosm of the universe. The sushumna also transmits the Kundalini energy (see pages 81 and 82) as it awakens from its sleep at the base of the spine.

MEDITATION ON GRACE

1 Sit cross-legged on the floor. Close your eyes and breathe in a slow, steady rhythm. Visualize opening the crown center at the top of your head and white light streaming in. On each in-breath, imagine drawing this energy down to the base of your pelvis. Hold your breath for a moment as the energy expands to fill your whole being.

2 With each slow out-breath, visualize drawing this light from your genitals and pelvis. As it moves up toward your crown, imagine the light flooding the energy centers located at your heart, throat and brow (the third eye).

3 Visualize the light streaming out of your crown and merging with the light streaming out of the head of anyone else you wish to include, so that the energy pools and unites. See yourself as a radiant being in a rainbow of light, linked to the divine.

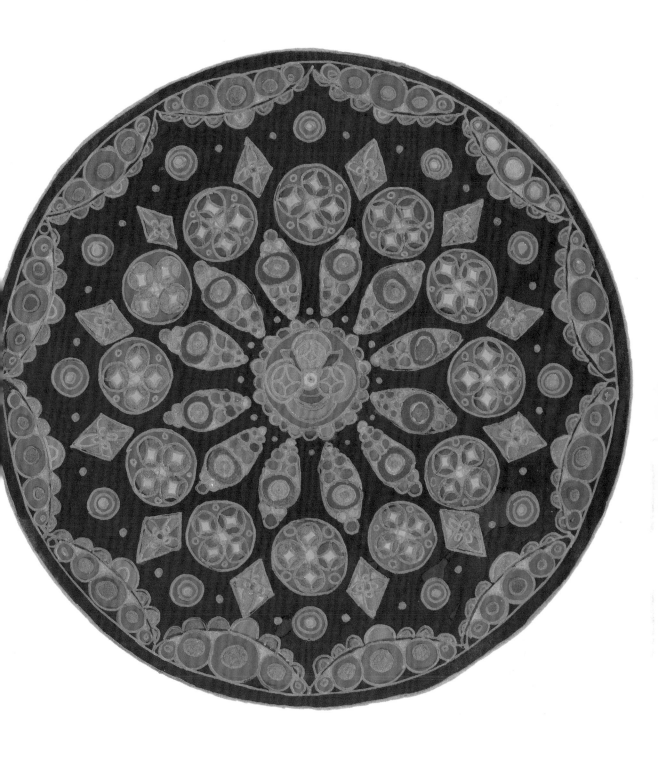

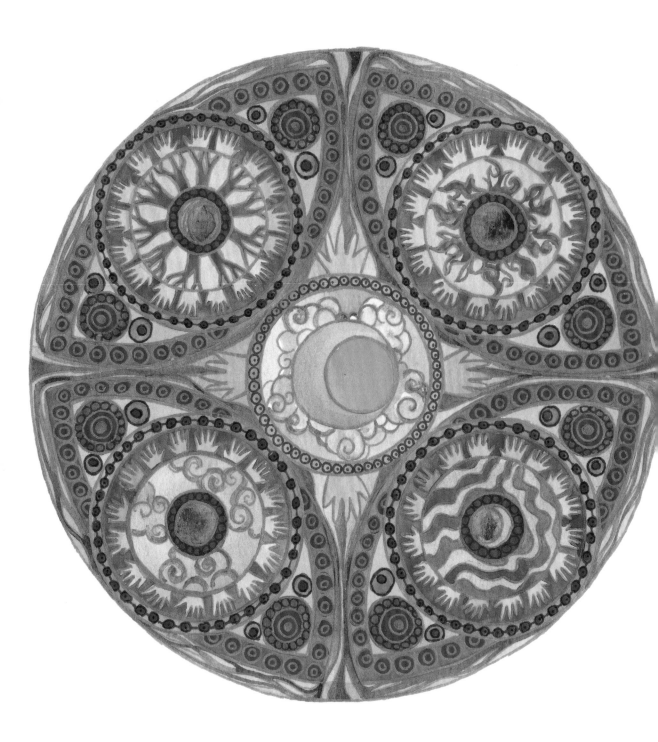

INTEGRATION

Carl Jung (see page 13) believed that our main task in life is to discover and fulfil our innate potential. The goal is to integrate all the disparate aspects of the self, even though it means tolerating the discomfort of increased self-knowledge.

JUNG IDENTIFIED FOUR basic psychological functions—thinking, feeling, sensing and intuition. He said that because in most people only one or two of these predominate, we need to develop the weaker functions. Also, because we all subconsciously attribute to other people negative aspects of ourselves that we don't want to acknowledge, Jung said that what we most dislike about others may indicate what we need to work on and integrate within our own psyche.

MEDITATION ON INTEGRATION

1 Gaze at the four quadrants of the mandala, while reflecting on the aspects of yourself that remain immature—that you would like to grow more. Think about what drives you crazy in others (perhaps you hate controlling or chaotic people, for example), and consider whether you have those same qualities yourself.

2 If your analytical mind tends to lose focus, practice focusing your attention throughout the day.

3 If you are insensitive to others, remind yourself throughout the day to prioritize your feelings—paying attention to your own and those of others.

4 If you deny your sensory information, give yourself a sensory diet of sensual input and stimulation.

5 If you tend to dismiss intuitive information, regularly stop to see if you are getting any instinctual information or knowledge about a situation.

IMPERMANENCE

Impermanence expresses the Buddhist notion that everything is constantly in flux, even planets, stars and gods. Cultivating an acceptance of the transitory nature of our current situation helps us deal with change and loss.

BECAUSE NOTHING LASTS, our natural reaction is to grasp on to people or experiences, but this can lead to emotional suffering. It is more healthy to learn to remain open to what comes into our lives and accept the situation when it leaves. We can become more adaptable and appreciative of the present moment. To do this, try to drop illusions and expectations, such as the direction of our own life and career, how we have imagined our parents' and siblings' life stories, our relationships, the need for someone to love us unconditionally and take care of us, our religious certainties, the kind of people we prefer our children to grow into, or our assumptions about health and longevity.

MEDITATION ON IMPERMANENCE

1 Think back to a time when you became aware you were holding on to an illusion. Recall your discovery that it was just an illusion, and remember how that felt.

2 Think about the new awareness that must have created the conditions for your realization that it was an illusion. What was the scenario that unfolded?

3 Relive the release when these illusions were dissolved.

4 Become aware of the spaciousness and sense of freedom you have when you live without illusions.

5 Let go of each and every one of your illusions, releasing them into the vast space of the universe.

GRIEF

You can never really lose someone close, as the good things that came out of the relationship will always stay with you. The experience of satisfying closeness has nourished you and you have incorporated it into your psyche.

YOUR HEART CAN be broken by many things, from difficult transitions to the loss of someone or something important. Loss of faith or trust may be huge and lead to you becoming defensive. To deal with grief, first acknowledge the depth of your loss and try to remain open to grief. The death of someone with whom you had a problematic relationship is especially difficult, as you won't have had a chance to heal the split. Remember that children who are grieving need to know as much as possible about what happened.

MEDITATION ON GRIEF

1 Honour what was good but let go. Acknowledge what that person or situation gave you, and consciously incorporate those qualities into yourself. If you felt loved, let the love in—the person has gone but the love hasn't. It is your love, and it has awakened love in you. Feel yourself becoming alive again. Let your energy reawaken.

2 Now become aware of what was troubled in the relationship. Bring to your inner eye their face or their energy, and visualize yourselves gazing at each other. Say whatever it is that still needs to be said. Imagine them hearing you say this and perhaps responding. Give them a memento to take with them. Embrace or say goodbye, and then in your mind's eye walk away.

3 Accept what is over, that it has gone and that there is space for new experiences and a new direction in your life.

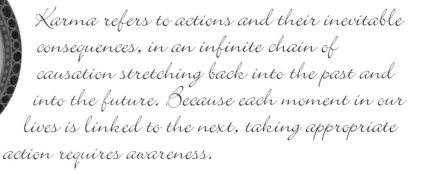

KARMA

Karma refers to actions and their inevitable consequences, in an infinite chain of causation stretching back into the past and into the future. Because each moment in our lives is linked to the next, taking appropriate action requires awareness.

THERE IS ALWAYS a consequence to every action, whether spiritual, mental or physical. If we speak in anger we will provoke an angry response. If we try to wound or manipulate, we will provoke a counter-attack. If we think unkind thoughts, we are likely to continue doing so. But if we generate loving thoughts, we are more likely to facilitate greater connection. Unfortunately, the ways we act can easily become habitual responses to situations, perpetuating unhealthy ways of thinking and acting, and limiting our ability to respond openly or positively to situations. We need to heal negative emotional habits in order to free ourselves of these destructive patterns, stopping the cycle of emotional pain and reactions.

MEDITATION ON KARMA

1 In your mind's eye, build up a fire in front of you. Watch the flames as they get stronger and stronger, until the fire is roaring.

2 Feel the energy of the fire in your own body, as if the flames were licking up your legs—not hurting you, but burning off any accumulated debris, leaving you clean and unscathed. Experience the flames as purifying, dissolving any negative karma from your inconsiderate actions or omissions from the past.

3 Imagine that you consign each and every thought and action that you regret on to the bonfire—your burning desire to transform these negative emotions.

PEACE

Peace is associated with restfulness, contentment, freedom and fulfilment. It describes a relationship of respect, justice and goodwill. For Mahatma Gandhi it was both a means and an end. Peace is a process, so we can create it each day in myriad ways.

PEACE SUGGESTS AN atmosphere of harmony and silence. If you are at peace with yourself you might describe yourself as feeling balanced, serene and calm. Inner peace is a state of mind, body and soul, an inner quality. Even in the midst of trauma or war, individuals may be able to maintain their state of inner peace. Use this meditation to help you to preserve your own sense of peace whenever you feel in need of it.

MEDITATION ON PEACE

1 Sit quietly, gazing at the mandala, reflecting how the dove has always been a messenger for peace. Even in the face of calamity, there is often an olive branch held out. Here the phoenix carries the message of reconciliation.

2 Look for the abode of peace within your own nature. Reach deep inside yourself to access a place of stillness. Acknowledge that you feel at peace with yourself. Let feelings of peace and harmony tranquilize your restlessness.

3 Accept your life as it is. Allow this feeling of peace to permeate your body, affecting those around you, soothing their distress.

4 In your mind's eye, imagine sharing this feeling with those you know and love. Send peace out into the community, sending out your intent to help harmonize all relationships between human beings. Extend your sense of peace and tranquillity to the natural world and the universe.

DEATH

An essential part of preparing for death is a review of life, looking at past joys and sorrows and saying goodbye to each experience. Death will be the ultimate letting go and, according to all spiritual traditions, this requires some practice.

MANY PEOPLE FACED with a terminal illness find that it releases a great rush of life-affirming energy, freeing them to explore avenues they had put off and to resolve unfinished emotional business. The awareness of death helps you live this day as if it were your last, letting go of distractions and the weight of accumulated sorrows. Many traditions have visualizations on death. Tantric iconography shows the god Shiva, meditating in the cremation ground, whitened with ashes, where the black goddess Kali reigns supreme. Kali stands for death, and her necklace of skulls reminds us of our ultimate destination.

MEDITATION ON DEATH

1 Let go of noises, distractions and thoughts. Let go of whatever pulls you out of a concentrated inner awareness.

2 Go inside yourself and become aware of all the things you are attached to. Let go of old emotions that hold you in thrall—remnants of joy and grief, connection and disillusionment, loyalty and bitterness, hope and sorrow. Let go of lingering resentment, frustration, need, pride, avarice. Let go of the past to allow more flexibility and responsiveness to the present.

3 Let go of the future—your drive and ambitions.

4 Do what you can do in any situation, and then let go.

5 Let go of pleasure as well as pain, and of seeking to prolong pleasure or to avoid pain. These limit our ability to go with the flow and to respond appropriately.

ANGER

Expressing your anger may temporarily relieve your pent-up frustration, but it just invites a hostile response. As the Buddha said, holding on to anger is like grasping a hot coal you plan to throw at someone else; you are the one who gets burned.

NOT KNOWING HOW to express anger, many people attempt to suppress it. However, it often eats away inside you, becoming toxic. Underneath anger are usually hurt, loneliness, fear or grief. This meditation teaches you to view all these emotions as different qualities of energy. Anger can arise from an ignorance of more effective ways of bringing change. By increasing understanding, you can transform your own negative feelings into a positive energy, as well as fostering reconciliation in people locked in conflict. Righteous anger can be positive, motivating you to take action, but it still needs to be directed. The Dalai Lama calls this "riding the bull", when you grasp the horns while riding the bull of your anger. Use this energy to fight against injustice, becoming effective and potent.

MEDITATION ON ANGER

1 Evoke your feelings of anger, bringing them into your conscious awareness. Allow yourself to experience anger instead of shying away from it. Can you feel that anger is pure energy?

2 Imagine yourself burning your anger in the crucible of the awareness of suffering, allowing the energy to be transformed into clarity of observation. You can see why and how contentious situations arise, and how unconscious behavior produces destructive energy.

3 Come to your own inner place of stillness, and cultivate the habit of holding on to your own conscious awareness in the midst of contention.

GUIDES

Think back to the people who have been important to you at different stages in life, and the varied ways they have guided you. Some mentors will have had a profound impact on you, perhaps even setting you in a different direction on your life journey.

WHETHER INTENTIONAL or not, true wisdom has been a light on your path. Some mentors were there with practical support, others with wise words, others leading by example. Each act or word of advice has helped sustain and nurture you. Acknowledge your right to need help, and celebrate the power of networks and the helping hand.

MEDITATION ON GUIDES

1 Look back over all the great and small kindnesses offered to you. Feel the warmth of these gifts in your heart. Feel the knowledge, purpose and perspective you have absorbed. They have helped you on your journey, just as you have guided others.

2 In the same way, you can offer yourself guidance. The aspects of you that are more evolved can offer a helping hand to the aspects of you that resist change or prefer distraction.

3 Know that you will find what you need, whether from the people around you or from within yourself. Feel sure that you will read a vital message at a time you are in need, or that you will have a conversation that helps you process some difficulty. You will attract into your life the people that you need as teachers, mentors and friends.

4 Bring to mind each mentor, including yourself, and inwardly offer your profound thanks and appreciation.

RITUAL

Many believe that creating rituals that affirm the sacred will encourage new, positive energies to manifest. This meditation shows how to create a ritual atmosphere while using a mandala. Choose a mandala from this book or make your own (see page 142).

RITUALS MAY INCORPORATE: • lighting candles • working with crystals • working with essences, flowers, perfumes, essential oils • setting up altars • praying to realized beings or deities • sacrificing personal luxuries or possessions • chanting and dancing • meditating on mandalas.

Before you start, clear any clutter and air the room. Lay out any refreshments you'll need. Add your preferred sensory stimuli. Prop up your chosen mandala on a book stand. We have provided a labyrinth for you to think about your own path to integration.

MEDITATION ON RITUAL

1 To create your own ritual using a mandala, close your eyes and go on an imaginary walk into a wooded place, following a path that traces a spiral or labyrinth, until it opens out into a circular clearing surrounded by shrubs. Within this space it is calm and silent.

2 You will not be disturbed, though you may be visited by creatures or spirits who have come to help you on your journey. Notice the images that come up as you enter this enclosed, sacred space, and be open to what unfolds.

3 Let your eyes run over the mandala, resting on details that claim your attention. This will help you enter your own sacred circle. Use the act of looking to enter into the mandala and become absorbed in its shapes, colors, reflections and associations.

CIRCLES OF CREATION: MAKING MANDALAS

ACCORDING TO THE WRITER JOSEPH CAMPBELL, the mandala is a means to align our own personal center, or circle, with "the universal circle". In the process of making a mandala, you become one with it, becoming more centered and achieving a sense of unification.

To make your own mandala, sit peacefully and quieten your mind. You may wish to use one of the preceding meditations as a starting point for the journey towards your own center. Use a geometry set to draw the outer circle, or simply trace around the outline of a bowl. With a light pencil divide the circle into quadrants (quarters) or into as many segments as seems appropriate and esthetically pleasing to you. Use these segments to structure your design, or superimpose free-form shapes over the top.

You can, of course, choose any motifs or symbols to represent pertinent themes in your life, but common themes include stars, crescent moons, suns, flowers such as a lotus or a rose, gods and demons, eggs, snakes and the shapes linked with the elements (earth, air, fire, water). Other possible designs include geometric shapes like triangles and diamonds, organic life forms, religious motifs and spontaneous free-form designs.

The chakra colors could be your palette: yellow/white, indigo, violet, green, yellow, orange, red. Certain colors have associations within tantra. White is masculine and stands for pefection, while red is feminine and dynamic. Orange is joyful and yellow is linked with the sun's energy. Green denotes nature, love and peace. Indigo represents the liminal – things that are invisible and transformational, at the edge of our waking consciousness. Violet is the color of imagination, inspiration and meditation, while pink denotes love and tenderness. Black is intangible and beyond consciousness. Silver is lunar and gold solar.

Similarly, use whatever materials inspire you and give you pleasure. People have made mandalas from watercolors, oil paint, chalk, sand, collage, felt, clay models, computer-generated images and much more. As regards style, feel free to be as literal and figurative, or as gestural and textural, as you like, allowing the mandala to emerge naturally.

Although the aim may be to create something that stimulates contemplation during a meditation, the process of making the mandala might, in itself, become your meditation.

INDEX

Further Reading

Bach, Richard, *Illusions: The Adventures of a Reluctant Messiah* (Arrow, 2001)

Bailey Cunningham, Lori, *Mandala: Journey to the Center* (DK Publishing, 2003)

Boorstein, Sylvia, *Pay Attention, for Goodness' Sake: Practicing the Perfections of the Heart–The Buddhist Path to Kindness* (Ballantine Books, 2002)

Campbell, Joseph, *The Hero with a Thousand Faces* (Princeton University Press, 1949)

Chodron, Pema, *When Things Fall Apart: Heart Advice for Difficult Times* (Element Books, 2005)

Chopra, Deepak, *The Path to Love: Spiritual Lessons for Creating the Love You Need* (Rider & Co., 1997)

Dalai Lama XIV, *Healing Anger: The Power of Patience from a Buddhist Perspective* (Snow Lion Publications, 1997)

Goodchild, Chloe, *The Naked Voice* (Rider & Co., 1993)

Huyser, Anneke, *Mandala Workbook* (New Age Books, 2006)

Jung, Carl G., *Man and His Symbols* (Picador, 1978)

Kornfield, Jack, *After the Ecstasy, the Laundry: How the Heart Grows Wise on the Spiritual Path* (Bantam Books, 2001)

Ladinsky, Daniel, *The Subject Tonight is Love: 60 Wild and Sweet Love Poems of Hafiz* (Pumpkin House, 1996)

Levine, Stephen, *A Year to Live* (Thorsons, 1997)

Lorius, Cassandra, *Tantric Sex: Making Love Last* (Thorsons, 1999)

Preece, Rob, *The Alchemical Buddha: Introducing the Psychology of Buddhist Tantra* (Mudra Publications, 2000)

Reps, Paul, and Senzaki, Nyogen, *Zen Flesh, Zen Bones: A Collection of Zen and Pre-Zen Writings* (Turtle Publications, 1998)

Rinpoche, Sogyal, *The Tibetan Book of Living and Dying* (Rider & Co., 2002)

Spezzano, Chuck, *If It Hurts, It Isn't Love* (Hodder Mobius, 2001)

Vessantara, *The Heart: The Art of Meditation* (Windhorse Publications, 2006)

Williamson, Marianne, *A Return to Love: Reflections on the Principles of a Course in Miracles* (HarperCollins, 1992)

Picture Credits